Beyond Blair

Prospects for a
New Socialist Left

A Chartist Publication

Edited by Chris Wearmouth

Chartist Publications
PO Box 52571, London EC2P 2XF
email: editor@chartist.org.uk
www.chartist.org.uk

Copyright © Chartist Publications 2006

ISBN-13 978-0-9515545-1-7
ISBN-10 0-9515545-1-4

Cover design by Mick Jones
Design and layout by David Floyd

CONTENTS

7 - Introduction - CHRIS WEARMOUTH

Section 1: Contemporary Analysis

14 - Beyond 'social justice' - Why changing the world is a socialist project - DON FLYNN

25 - Modernisation means democratisation - The importance of making Britain's public services genuinely accountable - MIKE DAVIS

36 - Sweet Harmony - Integration and the multi-cultural society are not incompatible - ANNA BLUSTON

42 - Bread first, then poetry - Or why socialism must remain anchored in reality - DON FLYNN

48 - On the cusp - Is a new global economic order inevitable? - FRANK LEE

Section 2: History

68 - Far from a one-trick ideology - A brief history of the libertarian socialist tradition - DUNCAN BOWIE

Section 3: Review

90 - Navigating the 'Third Road' - How accurate were the New Maps? - MARTIN COOK

Biographies

Anna Bluston is currently a primary school teaching assistant and part-time volunteer at the World Development Movement. She is twenty-five and currently lives in North-West London, but hopes to be moving somewhere else in the very near future. Her interests are destroying Capitalism through education and democratic means, watching T.V., and growing her nails.

Duncan Bowie is reviews editor of *Chartist*. He is also secretary of the South East London Fabian Society. He was a member of the Labour Party between 1975 and 2003, serving as a councillor from 1979 to 1983 in Oxford. He currently works as a principal strategic planner for the Mayor of London.

Martin Cook works in research in local government, has lived all his life in South London, and has degrees in social science and history. He is a lifelong member of C.A.M.R.A., Unison and predecessors, and of the Labour Party. He has been active in *Chartist* since 1970, writing on numerous topics from a 'sceptical Marxian' viewpoint.

Mike Davis has been *Chartist* editor for thirty-two years. For most of that time he has been a secondary school teacher in East London schools and latterly an education adviser. He has been a member of the Labour Party for thirty-three years.

Don Flynn has been active in socialist politics since 1968, when he started hanging around with dubious fellows in his hometown Liverpool. He's lived in London since 1970 and has been active in the Labour Party, trade union branch activities, legal advice services for working class communities, and various campaigns and organisations supporting the rights of immigrants.

Frank Lee was a mature student and read social sciences at New College Oxford and the London School of Economics. He was a lecturer for 18 years and is the author of *Fabianism and Colonialism*.

After a youth spent in various parts of the world (including Zimbabwe, Australia and Peterborough) **Chris Wearmouth** finally settled in Buckinghamshire and has just completed a degree in Politics, Philosophy and History at Birkbeck College, London. He regularly writes for *Chartist* and *Anticipations* – a Fabian Society journal – as well as various sporting organisations.

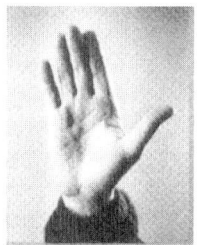 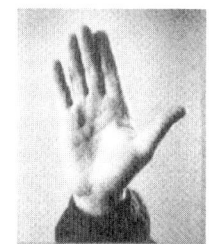 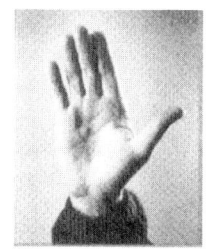

Introduction

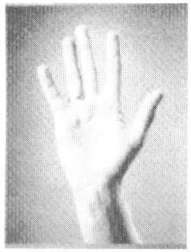 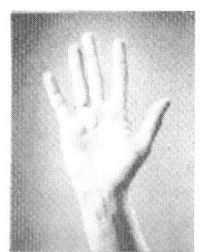 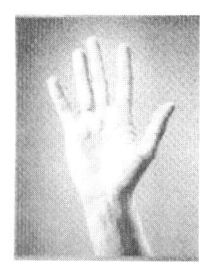

In 1990 a group of writers clustered around the left-wing publication *Chartist*, who had seen their beliefs and principles roughly overridden by the Conservative, specifically Thatcherite, juggernaut, collected together a series of essays that they believed could offer the way for socialism to present itself as the ideology to effect change for a better society for all.

In 2006, many of these same writers, upon seeing another heavyweight political personality do much the same as his Tory predecessor, have come together once more to restate how their principles are still as relevant as they were then. Indeed, how they are more important now than ever before.

At the time of *New Maps for the Nineties* socialism was at a crossroads. Sixteen years on the ideology is once more facing a crisis in finding its place in an increasingly 'middle of the road' society.

But whereas 1990's pamphlet came at the end of a decade of unprecedented upheaval in Britain – the Falkland's War, miners' strike, ongoing and deepening privatisation of the utilities, booms and busts – this publication comes a year into the third term of a government that has entrenched the Thatcherite policies of the preceding eighteen years. Unfortunately, amazingly, this administration has been in the hands of the Labour Party – specifically New Labour.

New Labour was a different animal to the fragmented, and therefore toothless opposition that sat opposite Margaret Thatcher when she was in her pomp. New Labour's remit was simple: become electable – not just once, but again and again and again and again. And it succeeded. In a middle-class commuter-belt school like my 'A'-Level alma mater, 8th May 1997 saw broad grins on the faces of the majority of those who had been able to vote, and the gentle ribbing of those true-blue (deluded, one might say) Conservatives willing to raise their head above the parapet.

Nine years on despondency has set in amongst the left. Indeed, as Rory Bremner says: "Tony Blair has become too right-wing for the Tories." An accurate summation.

In every sphere of government New Labour has introduced legislation that has disappointed as much as it has delighted those whose blood runs red rather than blue. True, more money than ever before has been invested in our school system. However, teachers are being forced ever more to justify their salaries and schools who have overstepped their budget are not being supported centrally, having to cut back spending in order to balance the books. And yes, there are more nurses within the National Health Service. But in many cases they are foreign workers who have been employed in Britain at the expense of their own health systems. Are these the actions of a truly socialist government?

Economically this country is strong, having ridden out global downturns that would previously have dragged us down with them. Furthermore, the decisions to make the Bank of England politically independent and adhering to Tory spending plans for the first two years after New Labour's 1997 victory were astute though controversial. On the other hand the free market's position is still as unshakable as it ever was during the 1980s and early-1990s. Admittedly, to bring the likes of British Gas or BT back into state ownership would be prohibitively expensive, although contributors here argue that new forms of democratic social ownership would be a more progressive course. However, the privatisation botch-job that is the railway system, which provided through the franchise system the perfect opportunity to bring the network back under the public umbrella, remains. Instead of not renewing franchises when they expired, thus ensuring that the massive amount of public subsidy could be directed entirely at the service rather than the shareholder (entirely justifiable and indeed potentially vote-winning), the government has chosen instead to offer longer franchises, albeit with smaller public handouts. Having said that, Stephen Byers's decision to pull the plug on Railtrack rather than pouring hundreds of millions of pounds into its financial black hole, was sound, leading as it has to an accountable and stable Network Rail.

Internationally the record is similar. The gains of the interventions in Sierra Leone and Afghanistan, together with the work of the Department for International Development under the stewardship of Claire Short (renowned overseas but woefully underplayed back home) have been undone by the tagging along with one of, if not the most unpopular and radical U.S. presidents in history. Iraq will hang over this Prime Minister in much the same way Vietnam did with Lyndon Johnson. The misjudgement of the invasion has been compounded ever since by the refusal to admit that we were wrong to break international convention to do so. Instead of being a shining light in helping the Afghans to build for the first time a genuine system of democratic government, and influencing the European Union to put genuine weight behind the Middle East peace process, New Labour is saddled with a reputation not as being interventionalist only when necessary, but as a party that has taken this country into more separate conflicts than any other.

The attitude towards the E.U. itself has been similarly muddled. The hard-line anti-Europe attitude of twenty years ago has been reversed completely into a policy that recognises the need for the U.K. to be at the heart of the Union, for trade as well as political purposes. Yet instead of taking the opportunity of explaining why E.U. regulation is a necessary and integral part of making us stronger, why the reform of the E.U. proposed by the Constitution – not that radical, by the way – was to the betterment of all of us, Blair's government instead shied away from the tough fight, leaving the goal wide open for the vocal anti-E.U. right-wing to pass the ball into the net and win that particular game. Again, instead of being at the vanguard of the European argument, New Labour is regarded as having principles built on sand rather than any genuine belief that the E.U. is the best way forward.

However, the malaise socialism finds itself in has deeper roots than one powerful man's personal commitment and conviction.

It is well documented that we are living in a world considerably different to that of sixteen years ago, socially as well as politically. We are better connected, more informed – if we want to be – more able to travel and engage with the world. The internet and advent of digital satellite programming platforms have brought with them a plethora of media 'competition' for our attention. 'Competition' is in quotes because in the same way as Twix, Snickers and Mars all come from the same manufacturer, and Ariel and Persil both have their profits head to the same bunch of shareholders, many of the channels offered on Sky are owned by a relatively small number of corporations. Similarly, outside of the major centres of population, 'local' radio is generally in the hands of two organisations – the B.B.C. and GCap – and 'regional' newspapers are owned by companies such as Johnston Press. Yet the veneer of 'choice' and 'competition' is so strong that comparatively few actually know to whom their chocolate, detergent or television and radio station of choice actually belongs to.

Indeed, the greatest competition the world sees at present is in international politics, where the United States and European Union are facing economic threats from the growing powerhouses of India and China. The latter in particular offers a state-controlled capitalism that both supports the US Government's spiralling debt burden and provides the cheap goods to ensure that the likes of Wal-Mart can see their bottom line fatten.

Domestically the social fragmentation seen in the so-called 'real world' has been reflected in politics. Never before have so many identified so little with the established party system. That is not to say that Joe Public has become disenfranchised or embittered with political issues. The millions who took to the streets against the invasion of Iraq and hundreds of thousands that marched to try and avert the hunting ban – many who took part in both demonstrations had never before shown their displeasure with government policies in such a manner – attest to that. Europe; gun violence; the N.H.S.; education. Up and down the country these and many other issues provoke debate in a variety of public forums, be they radio phone-ins, the letters pages of local newspapers or the newest form of expression, the internet blog.

No, the disenchantment is not with single issues; it is with the system itself. This is why an ideology such as socialism – or indeed neo-liberalism – that seeks to impose itself across the policy spectrum finds itself increasingly marginalized. Some aspects are supported by the majority, such as the provision of a universal health system free at the point of use. But to impose a particular hospital on a patient simply because they live in a certain post-code won't find similar favour. Especially if the hospital two miles further away in the opposite direction has a regional monopoly on the best cancer doctors, for example. Yet to concentrate on 'beacon' hospitals or schools, as this administration is intent on doing, in an attempt to generate regional innate competitive instincts in order to raise standards, is less preferable than any genuine attempt at raising standards in every discipline in every hospital and school.

The struggle faced by socialism is how to answer the question of relevance. How can a single political ideology, particularly one that brings with it the baggage of history – the radicalism of the 1980s is still within living memory for many – offer a comprehensive programme that is palatable to the majority? After all, for an ideology to genuinely succeed it must not just appeal to a select few – it must appeal to enough people to achieve power in Westminster. Little change was effected purely from the sidelines.

This pamphlet is the demonstration by *Chartist* writers that socialism not only has a place in twenty-first century Britain, but can also provide a genuine alternative platform and path to the one presently undertaken by the Labour Party.

Beyond Blair is split into three sections. It opens with a series of articles analysing the contemporary political situation socialism finds itself in. Firstly, Don Flynn deals with the legacies of Blairism. Tony Blair may not be the architect of New Labour, but he was the project's public face and therefore one could assume that without him the party would not have gained such a majority in 1997, nor retained so much of it in 2001 and 2005. Indeed, it has been overlooked by some that a sixty-something majority would previously have been regarded as something of a landslide. But Blair, instead of being treated as a hero, has rapidly become something of a pariah. Whether he was ever a genuine socialist remains open to question, but there is no doubt that if socialism can regain the party it must deal with Blair's not inconsiderable legacy.

Mike Davis argues why the public sector must be democratised in order to truly modernise. One of the principles of the Chartist movement was the right to vote – albeit for men over the age of 21 – and yet those who work in the public services have less say, less input into the way their work is organised and implemented. The much vaunted, and necessary, modernisation programme has been, in his words, 'clamped with a myriad of consultants, private finance initiatives, business principles and market systems.' Yet this is not the only solution. Worker ownership and good management and delivery of services are not incompatible.

Anna Bluston discusses the ever-growing question of culture and immigration of how socialists should embrace it (or otherwise). With birth rates declining, immigration is necessary in order for our economy to continue to grow. Not only that, but recent arrivals are taking on the roles that the British young would previously have done. For example, in any large town or city you would be hard-pressed to find a restaurant or cleaning company that does not have recent arrivals performing the most menial jobs. But this continuing influx creates an ever increasing potential for a culture clash that will define the next few years.

Finally, Don Flynn and Frank Lee present their views of economic development. The global market is not going away in the foreseeable future, but it has created an economic chimera that threatens to overwhelm all. Therefore the question is 'what follows the meltdown?' We are on the verge of a new global economic order – what British socialists must do is figure out what their place in it should be.

The second section is Duncan Bowie's history of the libertarian tradition *Chartist* promotes and upholds. As he writes: '*Chartist* is not only part of the democratic socialist tradition: it is part of a libertarian tradition. In contrast with the anarchist tradition, we do see a role for the state...but we also recognize that the power of the state should be limited and the liberties of individuals protected so far as they do not conflict with the liberties of others.' Though the Chartist movement was British, many of the influences for both itself and socialism as a whole came from overseas, even if Karl Marx is buried in Highgate Cemetery. Furthermore, as with much of today's geo-politics, without paying heed to history we cannot truly seek to avoid falling into the same pitfalls or share the same successes.

The final section is Martin Cook's appraisal of *New Maps for the Nineties*. In order for us to ascertain the position we find ourselves in today, it is important – necessary, even – to know where we stood in 1990 and how different the situation is today. Communism may have been swept away – at least in Europe – but capitalism has not provided all the solutions either.

Some say that the foreign influence is still the guiding light – be it continental social democracy or American 'Third Way' universalism. We think otherwise, and present *Beyond Blair: Prospects for a New Socialist Left* as a demonstration of how British socialism can not just recapture the soul of Labour, but be a genuine alternative to the malaise.

Chris Wearmouth, June 2006

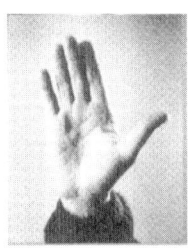 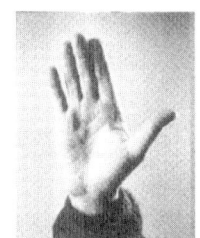 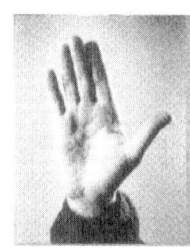

Section 1: Contemporary analysis

New Labour is an inherently modern political animal. The 'Third Way' has reshaped the old boundaries, including in its canon guiding principles seeking perpetual success.

But what exactly is the legacy being bequeathed on Labour by one Anthony Charles Lynton Blair? How are the dual challenges of public service reform and increased cultural integration to be successfully managed? And what can socialists do in order to prepare themselves for the anticipated reshaping of the global economic order?

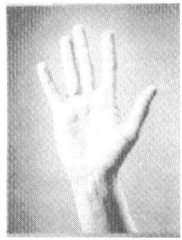 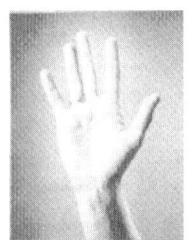 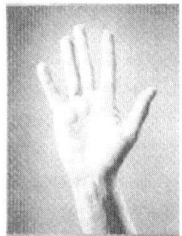

Beyond 'social justice'

Why changing the world is a socialist project

Don Flynn

A large part of the discussion about Tony Blair and the legacy he has sought to bequeath to politics has been about the compatibility of his ideas with the traditions of the Labour Party. For some the New Labour project is simply a continuation of the revisionism which has always been a major component of the Party's intellectual life, with political thinkers and active politicians of the order of Hugh Dalton, Evan Durbin, Douglas Jay, Tony Crosland and Hugh Gaitskell, all setting out a formidable stall for post-Marxist social democracy.

For others, including some who have themselves been ploughing the revisionist furrow for decades, Blair is a politician who has moved beyond social democracy and should be more properly understood, and excoriated, as a European-style Christian Democrat, advocating, as he does, a pro-capitalist economic programme which limits the social part of its politics to calling on business to operate more ethically.

The principal reason why Blair is deemed to have taken New Labour beyond social democracy is his abandonment of the principle of equality as being the touchstone of his politics. For all the revisionists hitherto, with Crosland making the most famous case in his *The Future of Socialism*, progress meant constructing counterweights to the polarising effects of capitalism, in the form of institutions such as comprehensive education, a national health service and a redistributive tax and social security system, which would allow the essential equality of citizens to be asserted as the basis for social solidarity. Though a vast gulf separated the old Labour right from its Marxian-influenced counterparts on the left, common agreement on the centrality of egalitarianism marked out the terrain on which those who adhered to the approach of the Labour Party expected to do battle with the representatives of capital.

There is an argument that the essential elements of a commitment to egalitarian politics have been retained in the politics of New Labour, though no longer expressed in terms of a doctrinal commitment in the manner of the old Labour Party. Narrowed down to the issue of equality of opportunity, in its Blairite version, the task of progressive politics is to ensure that citizens are no longer prevented by virtue of the social class of their birth, their ethnicity, gender or sexual orientation are impediments to obtaining a good education or the prospect of a successful career in employment or running a business.

This limited aspiration for equality was not considered good enough by the earlier proponents of social democratic politics. The need to secure equal opportunities was certainly a start, but if beyond that the statistics still showed that children born to working class parents, despite access to better standard education, were likely to remain in low-paid and low-esteemed employment, then a more critical searchlight had to be directed on the institutions of the labour market and society in general to discover why this was the case. For the older generation of democratic socialists, equal opportunity meant little if it could not be demonstrated to have generated greater equality of outcome.

But even here New Labour's champions have a response. The issue of where people end up in life is no longer amenable, they say, to the type of social and economic policy interventions used by Labour governments after the Second World War or in the 1960s and 1970s because the character of our post-Fordist economy has become so immensely complex. The diversity of life-styles and patterns of consumption and the interactions between the various parts of the global division of labour now means that the unintended consequences arising from particular policy initiatives are likely to be greater than those intended. Poorly constructed attempts to eradicate low pay, for example, will be reacted against in labour markets which can utilise the mobility of the factors of production more effectively than ever before, to result in capital flight, outsourcing or the replacement of one group of workers with newly-arriving migrants.

For New Labour the reduction of poverty, which it certainly favours, has to be re-thought of as being less a matter of economic policies as of ethical practices. In this assertion Blairite thinkers claim a part of the legacy of the social democratic revisionists who, following Crosland, insisted that socialism had to be considered as a value judgment rather than a commitment to the interests of a particularly social class. Building on this insight the concept of 'social justice' has emerged as the template for New Labour thinking in which all issues of social and economic place can be located.

Social justice functions for New Labour as a claim on the ruling, hegemonic ideas of contemporary society in pretty much the way intended by the Italian Marxist political thinker Antonio Gramsci when he set out his ideas in his prison notebooks under the reign of Mussolini's fascism. All the currents of commonsensical thinking are required to relate to it in some shape or form, whether they be conservative, liberal or socialist in orientation, and in the context of a debate abut the attainment of social justice the superiority of one or another of these political approaches is likely to be proven.

An example of a way in which social justice was used in this Gramscian-way (though this was almost certainly not its intention) might be found in the work of the Commission on Social Justice set up when John Smith was the leader of the Labour Party, under the chairpersonship of Sir Gordon Borrie. Its 1994 report 'Social Justice – Strategies for National Renewal', set out a vision for modernisation which it termed 'Investors' Britain'. Aiming to combine the 'ethics of community' with 'the dynamics of a market economy', the report purported to demonstrate linkages along a long chain in which the welfare and quality of life of all citizens was connected with economic prosperity at the national level. The need for a strong welfare state was insisted on as laying close to the heart of Investors' Britain, with its value being demonstrated primarily through gains achieved at the level of economic efficiency rather than, as might have been seen by the Bevanite pioneers of the post-war period, as a continuation of the forward march of the working class movement.

But the most impressive achievement of the Borrie report lay in the way in which it set out an approach to politics based on consensus and commonsense, it also marked out the ways in which political tension and conflict would continue to exist even within the social justice framework. There remained most obviously a conservative approach to social justice that would oppose the efforts of central government to usurp the prerogatives it believed properly belonged to civil society and individuals exercising free choice. Battle would be done with the advocates of 'Deregulators' Britain', but with more chance of success if it took place on the terrain of social justice rather than the traditional doctrines of economic management policies on which old Labour had staked its claim to superiority over the Tories.

The social justice agenda has remained the defining feature of the New Labour approach and its success in marking out the hegemonic terrain of early twenty-first century politics should be acknowledged. This is particularly the case at a time when politics across the U.K. is in the process of reconfiguring itself around the issues New Labour would insist were the pieces of its own core agenda. The election of

David Cameron to the leadership of the Conservative Party and the political discussions he has attempted to initiate is an obvious example of these types of development.

But after eight years of New Labour governance, and at the point where Blair himself is at the point of bowing out of power, it is reasonable to ask just how robust the experiment in Third Way politics has been, and whether it really does provide a template for progressive politics in the twenty-first century. Whilst it can be acknowledged that the rhetoric of political debate has changed in the years since 1997 when New Labour was elected to office, and that important policy objectives such as the eradication of poverty, the strengthening of social cohesion, and a humanitarian interest in the plight of the developing world has been advanced, this record has also been blighted by a dependency on the ethos of private enterprise and free market capitalism which has certainly limited, if not flatly contradicted, efforts to achieve greater levels of social justice.

Whatever success New Labour has had in shifting the centre towards the rhetoric of social justice is counterbalanced by the absence of clear evidence of progress on the substantive policy issues. The two volumes auditing the record of New Labour in government at the 2001 and 2005 stages by Polly Toynbee and David Walker, despite the often-professed sympathy for the New Labour project on the part of the authors, still set out accounts which showed a deep ambiguity of outcomes in which claim for targets achieved and positive statistical evidence were open to disputation by the array of experts who alone are equipped with the skills to make head or tail of the claims as on how the country changed during these years.

Beyond the journalism of Toynbee and Walker, amongst ordinary citizens enthusiasm for politics has shown itself to be in drastic and dangerous decline, with participation in party-based activities dwindling to levels close to the inert and even voting becoming a bit of business which only sixty per cent or thereabouts of the population can be bothered with.

The oft-discussed alienation of citizens from traditional forms of politics should really be understood as a product of the 'what works' principle which New Labour set out as the basis of its opposition to political doctrine in the early days of the 'Blair revolution'. The core idea here reflected something of the frustration of parliamentary politicians who felt their scope for policy initiative was too often restrained by the need to fit in with an ideological sense of what the mission of a party of the left actually was. Historically this had been associated with advancing the cause of the working class in society, though policies which favoured the realm of the public, rather than the private world of domestic and private interests. An identification with macro-economic planning and the redistribution of wealth through public services and social security emerged as the touchstone of the democratic socialist doctrine, which required political representatives to discipline their thinking and actions to advance these general approach.

Blair's opposition to this style of politics was presented as a positive assertion of the merits of sensible pragmatism, of a desire to find by hook or crook the best way to achieve agreed objectives, and not be constrained by outmoded assumptions about the 'correct' way of doing politics. If a thorough consideration of the problems of schools policy, for example, established the fact that enterprising head teachers were too often held back from doing good things by the bureaucracy of local education authorities, then no sentimental attachment to notions of local planning of resources to meet the priority needs of a wider community would be allowed to stand in the way of the remedies needed.

But even here there were choices to be made which reveal the obvious fact that, whatever they claim to the contrary, politicians invariably allow their supposedly pragmatic decision-making to be guided by a priori assumptions about the normative functioning of social existence. If the problem was moribund educational authorities constraining enterprising head teachers, then one solution might have been the reorganisation of the authorities to bring imagination and enterprise into their ranks. This has not been the direction favoured by New Labour.

The fact is New Labour does operate with a commitment to a normative ideological framework as a guide to its decision-making, but it is one that operates on very different principles than that developed by the democratic socialist movement. Profoundly hostile to the idea that the public realm can itself be the source of enterprise, New Labour has consistently demonstrated a deep attachment to the viewpoint which became entrenched under Margaret Thatcher, that innovation and dynamism were properties possessed solely by the private sector. It was only when private sector operatives could be persuaded to engage with a social policy issue that real innovation could be expected to take and change forced to come about. With this idea guiding almost all their policy thinking, whether dealing with education, the health services, public transport, environmental or social security issues, New Labour has shown a persistent bias in favour of strategies aimed a securing the involvement of the private sector which go well beyond its claimed pragmatic adaptation to so-called new realities.

The mechanism for securing private sector involvement has been the creation of opportunities for profit making in areas of social policy to which had previously structurally excluded this possibility. The Public Finance Initiatives (P.F.I) developed by the Conservative government developed greater momentum under New Labour as private companies assumed roles in building and running everything from hospitals and schools to prisons, railway lines and public highways. This deeply mixed results of P.F.I across all the areas of their use, ranging from the scandalous bad to the merely indifferent performance of private sector management is offset to some extent by the headline grabbing strategy of positively spinning photo-opportunities for ministers to appear outside brand-new, state-of-the-art facilities which, the public are assured, would never have been brought into existence had not the private sector been involved.

But the ability of citizens to make clear-cut judgments on New Labour reforms is further obfuscated by the ideological role of the 'choice' agenda. Ushered in alongside the promise of large-scale investment in public services, 'choice' has the function of securing a consumerist commitment on the part of the citizens to the renewal of the sector. The private sector model holds out the alluring prospect of a diverse range of services being created giving users the opportunity to exercise preferences for one over the other. New Labour's political imagination finds it difficult to imagine any other basis for attaining the support of citizens other than giving free reign to calculations of the personal benefits likely to accrue to them.

In taking this position the government and its supporters both underestimate the difficulty in achieving the levels of choice exhibited in the private sector, and also the capacity of citizens to think politically about the services they are receiving, and to be able to defer personal gratification in appropriate circumstances in the interests of a greater public good.

On the first point, the problem arises from the fact that public sector utilisation of resources typically runs at levels greater than ninety per cent (in the cases of such services as hospitals, schools and prisons) whilst private enterprise operates at much lower levels of usage. This happens because at any particular time the private sector will consist of not only efficient firms with high levels of resource utilisation, but also new enterprises who are still striving to maximise their market potential and also inefficient companies which, if they fail to restructure, will go out of business in due course. But across the range of different levels of activities sufficient capacity exists to provide customers with choices in the services or range of products available.

The public sector, on the other hand, does not operate on this basis because there is no general expectation of less successful services going out of business or being closed down on the same market principles. Services are planned for and financed on the assumption that they will operate at optimal levels of efficiency across all their units, and unused capacity therefore tends to be squeezed out the system. Admittedly New Labour talks about a management ethos in the public sector tolerating the closure of units deemed to be operating at less than optimal level, and some schools and hospitals have already been put in this position. But the option of closure is always discussed as a mechanism to be used in exceptional circumstances, as a means of punishing consistently poor performance rather than a routine market mechanism facilitating closures, bankruptcy, acquisition and asset stripping on a daily basis.

In absence of the existence of high levels of spare capacity which would allow the exercise of choice to be meaningful for all citizens, the rhetoric around the issue has become a cover under which some advantaged citizens are able to corner whatever opportunities might exist for preference and to monopolise this to their own advantage. The choice agenda has by these means become a tool allowing for the enhancement of, typically, middle class segments to the detriment of working class citizens.

But is this inevitable? Researchers and policy analysts have demonstrated over a long period of time that the middle classes drawn a disproportionate benefit from public sector services even in the more egalitarian conditions which prevailed in earlier decades. The point for democratic socialists however, is not that middle class people should be disadvantaged by a positive strategy for the public services, but that the system operates in such a way as to maximise the potential for the best level of service provision to cascade downwards and across to all. This happens whenever local middle class commitment to particular facilities, whether they be schools, health centres, libraries or such things as parks, playing fields or footpaths, where the effect of optimal levels of utilisation is to maximise the benefits available to the whole of the local community. A bustling, busy health centre, for example, is a place in which the opportunities for the provision of a range of health services, from health screening, influenza inoculation campaigns, through to public talks on safe sex or better diet are all very much greater.

A political framework for the development of public services in this way is necessary and its supporters cannot rely on an appeal to pragmatic claims for 'what works' anymore than New Labour has been able to do. If there are good reasons for believing that the PFI/consumer choice model cannot succeed in driving reform then an alternative approach will be needed. One consistent with the commitment and values of democratic socialism is that of 'civic republicanism', which ironically New Labour has been prepared to consider, but more in the realm of the imposition of social discipline than the provision of social benefits.

Civic republicanism is rooted in the understanding that the values underpinning the coherence and cohesion of society are more extensive and complex than those generated by the presumptions of consumerism operating in free markets. Intergenerational solidarity, for example, the respect which the young owe to the old and vice versa, is not generally supported by market relations, which on the contrary are more likely to regard deference to the interests of others as an impediment to the saturation of the ego-driven desire for personal gratification. The social obligation to afford respect to all the people who inhabit the social space of modern cities exists not because of intimate knowledge of their personalities (the great majority will, after all, remain relative strangers to one another) but in the political understanding that our societies are complex, frequently impersonal, and that consequently a decent standard of life is only possible if we implicitly agree on the need to behave in a generally civilised way to one another. Whilst these obligations extend to relations in commercial dealings they do not have a particularly strong purchase there, precisely because the tension and clash of individual material interests is heightened in activities where we are concerned to make money or cut the best possible deals, possibly at the direct expense of the person we are dealing with. As a general rule, for respect and the meeting of mutual obligations to one another to be maximised, the realm of market-based economic activities should be curtailed as much as possible.

Some within the New Labour camp have taken up some ideas around republican politics on the grounds that it contained an appeal to social discipline requiring citizens to exercise civic responsibility as a condition for receiving rights and benefits. A programme promoting 'active citizenship' has been seen as providing a balm, healing divisions generated by social polarisation and the negative effects of diversity. The concept of citizenship used here is essentially one designed from above by policy-makers and offered to the population with inducements of various sorts for those choosing to buy into the approach. Public honours have been overhauled to allow for the nomination of 'community heroes' – people who have some claim to providing good service to the Commonwealth who would serve as role models for others. A public debate about the meaning of citizenship itself was initiated during the course of the 'Big Conversation' exercise in 2003, intending to produce a consensus on what British national identity entails for public order and social discipline. The business of integrating immigrants into British society was also overhauled, with greater emphasis placed on the symbolic trappings of naturalisation into citizenship as a rite of passage. At the most draconian extreme of this approach, the government has placed legislation on the statute book which would allow some people to be stripped of their British citizenship if they were considered by ministers to have acted in serious breach of what would normally be hope for from a 'good' citizen.

But the appropriation of the rhetoric of citizenship for the limited purposes of policing good behaviour and law and order is at best a feeble use of the potential of a republican political ethic to sustain a disciplined social ethic. In the absence of a serious attempt to locate an ethic of citizenship within the context of democratic renewal and the development of cooperative and collectivist enterprise and endeavour, the citizenship debate looks like little more than 'nanny state' politicians lecturing the people on how they should behave better and more responsibly. As such it seems unlikely to achieve very much against the tide of public moods which, feeding on consumer-binge fuelled egoism, is clearly encouraging people to move in precisely the opposite direction than greater social responsibility.

It is worthwhile thinking more deeply about the use of the concept of civic republicanism, which New Labour deals with in only the most superficial way. This tradition in politics assumes that the realm of the public needs to be consciously maintained through policies which protect it from encroachment by private interests, which take such forms of corruption as bribery or the pursuit of private gain from public office. Power which has its roots in the public realm should ideally be divided along the functions of the legislature, executive and judiciary, and accountability maintained through frequent periodic elections and the legally enforceable right to information. Power should be understood as a social relationship existing between citizens who understand that the pursuit of individual happiness needs to be balanced by proper regard for the public good. Unlike monarchical systems of governance, an effort is made to dissociate the exercise power from the mystifications of charisma or rights sanctioned by obscure deities. Neither should it be sentimentalised by presumptions of the existence of abstractions like 'the nation' or 'national interest' in which complex relations of power are dissolved into simplicities given life and meaning by emotional identification with collective life.

The civic republican entity should therefore be small enough to allow the relationships of governance to be transparently rational in their operation. A written constitution will assist in securing these conditions, but this should not be framed in a way rendering the civic entity rigid and incapable of adaptation. Importantly, participation in the life of the republic should be in accordance with a strong ethos of public service.

However, beyond the insistence of the importance of critical ideas dealing with public enterprise and civic republican values into the movements for the reform and renewal of society, a discussion of the contribution likely to be made by democratic socialist movements also needs to consider the continued relevance of the vexed question of class to this project.

The troubled legacy of Marxism here brings obvious difficulties to the way in which we should consider the question of class. Marx himself constructed a destiny for the working class which construed a mission based on ontological reasoning. From this standpoint the conditions of existence of the modern proletariat were considered to common interests for members of this class, the pursuit of which created the conditions for the overthrow of capitalism and the creation of a better society in the form of socialism. It is difficult nowadays to accept the proposition that workers are destined to act as the 'universal class' destined to abolish all conditions of oppression and exploitation, and only a dogmatist would attempt to do so.

But aside from the romanticism of the traditional Marxian claim on the destiny of the working class there is a sense in which socialism must continue with its identification of project of radical reform with a close organic connection with the working class movement. This concerns firstly the historical fact that much social and political progress during the past two centuries is closely associated with the rise of an organised labour movement in Britain and elsewhere. During the periods when the leadership of the working class has identified its interests with those of political and social reform the greatest and most rapid advances towards social justice have been made. The issue for the contemporary socialist movement is whether the conditions currently existing in global politics have the potential for re-kindling amongst workers the sense of purpose and solidarity that allowed progress to be made in the past. It will be submitted here, but without the space to argue the point in detail, that the lives of working class people across the world are lived out in conditions which, if properly addressed, would reignite the solidarity and purpose which could again result in concrete gains and achievements.

But there is another reason why modern-day socialists should continue in their practical political work to secure the closes possible identification with working class interests. This is the same reason that was argued by democratic socialist thinkers of the stature of G.D.H. Cole back in the '30s when he warned against radical reformist politics based on the good ideas and political enthusiasms of the middle class intelligentsia. Without a standard which would allow favoured policies to be measured against their potential impact on the conditions of life of working class people there would be no way of knowing whether our ambitions would lead to improvements or disasters for the great mass of people in society. Socialism as a politics intimately related to the interests of the working class is therefore essential to stop radicalism from becoming something relating exclusively to the interests of the middle classes.

There is much that suggests that this has been the precise fate of the brand of Labour Party revisionism that began life in the re-thinking done in the face of the defeats inflicted by the Thatcher and Major governments over a period of two decades, and which have ended up as the New Labourism espoused by the group which remains directly around Tony Blair. The evidence is that this has not provided the robust basis for re-thinking and re-launching a modern centre left politics, and it now seems destined to dwindle away into an ill-defined 'progressivism' which identifies progress with U.S.-style political economy and social standards.

The challenges which lie in the immediate future, extend from the protection of working class interests in the modern, deregulated workplace, through to the renewal of the welfare state, the advancement of political democracy and human rights, and mesh in with the global challenges of development and the eradication of poverty abroad, the construction of a global economy which reconciles human productive activity with the protection of the biosphere in which we all depend. If progress is to be made in the fulfilment of these objectives a renewed and reinvigorated socialist movement will be essential.

Modernisation means democratisation:

The importance of making Britain's public services genuinely accountable

Mike Davis

Tony Blair's government is losing its way on modernisation. The enormous majorities bequeathed to New Labour by the British people in response to years of Tory rule are being squandered. It all started such promise with devolution in Scotland and Wales, restoration of London government, the Human Rights Act, modernising public services and a more communitarian form of regeneration. This was the New Deal for Communities, the New Labour alternative to the Tories Single Regeneration Budget that aimed at bringing local people into decision-making about which projects are to be funded and how they are to be developed and managed.

Few would dispute the need for reform and modernisation. Public services had become bureaucratic and remote from consumers. Often providers, be they refuse collectors, local government officers, or health workers, appeared to lose sight of service users through the growth of a hierarchical structure or the view of 'management' as a private-sector type employer. Though the public service ethos at the heart of public services still breathes it has now been clamped with a myriad of consultants, private finance initiatives, business principles and market systems. Blair did toy with idea of communitarianism following Amitai Etzioni, with mutualism and a third sector of voluntary style provision, but these approaches also seem to have died a death or been buried in the pursuit of the private as the panacea.

The strength of New Labour was to identify the weakness in post-war, and even pre-war Labour thinking which was dominated by a Fabian top-down, bureaucratic/administrative approach to socialism and the state. The dominant idea, pursued by the Attlee and Wilson governments of the three decades after the Second World War was very much that the state was a neutral body and that, in the form of government, civil services, local government and quangoes, the state would take over from private industries and services.

Labour's 1945 Manifesto *Let Us Face the Future* continued the nationalising command economy approach of the war years. Public ownership and Morrisonian municipalism (after the London Labour leader and post-war Home Secretary) was the rallying cry. The Bank of England, fuel and power, transport, iron and steel were all to be nationalised, the National Health Service (N.H.S.) was formed and even land nationalisation was planned. For a short period the changes appeared to work in kick-starting the economy and rebuilding war-ravaged cities and industries and services. The N.H.S., state schools free for all, public housing, local education authorities (LEAs – created 40 years earlier), railways, post, and the basic utilities – gas, electric, water – all came out of private hands. True, enormous compensation was being paid to the old private owners, which drained the Exchequer and limited the flexibility of the state to assist in developing public services.

But the other more fundamental problem was that social relation of provision did not change. What was missing was the democratic element. This became increasingly evident throughout the 1950s and 1960s. The Wilson and Callaghan governments grappled with the problem but found no solution. In industry the 1977 Bullock Report proposed a radical reform and greater participation of workers in management. The report was left on the shelf. The Social Contract with the trade unions was sabotaged by government inaction on the social wage following Tony Crosland's announcement that "the party's over", and that no new money would go into public services. Of course some trade unions refused to break out of narrow sectional interests, pursuing differentials and opposing pay policies. But elsewhere little changed. Consumers and workers were increasingly frustrated by the inability of core services to deliver high quality, appropriate and accessible services when needed, opening the door to almost twenty years of right-wing Tory government, during which time the erosion of the public and promotion of the individual and private as solutions grew apace. Much of the left fell into a narrow economist view that it was all about wages or funding and failed to question some of the core problems of the public sector. This is where New Labour came in.

However, Blair and Gordon Brown's waste of opportunities and trust is visible no more starkly than in the area of the public: specifically public services where the rallying cry of modernisation and reform has sunk into a dogmatic pursuit of the market and spurious notions of choice as the only means to change.

Following hard on the heels of the inventions of the John Major years, the Private Finance Initiative (P.F.I.) and Public Private Partnerships comes the idea of co-payment. This wheeze dreamed up by Blair and ex-Minister Peter Mandelson is not a new idea, but, reports Alyson Pollock, essentially uses changes 'already an everyday experiences for the old and frail the disabled and most who need dental and optical care'.

In a *Guardian* feature entitled 'Selling off by stealth is here to stay', Pollock argues that since government policy is that it matters not who provides the service as long as it is publicly funded, no public service is protected from the spectre of private profit-making. Whether it be rail, post, healthcare, pensions or education the process of commodification and privatisation unfolds.

Not to be outdone, ex-*Marxism Today* columnist Charlie Leadbetter extols the virtues of individual choice and personalisation of public services as the route to reform. This neatly avoids the issue of improving quality for all. What is important is that your local hospital, school or council can provide an appropriate and successful service. Parents don't want to have to move or bus their children miles to exercise choice. Personalisation has merit if it means differentiation and tailored services within the universal to meet a pupil's special education needs or aptitudes, for example, but not if it means undermining the quality of neighbouring provision by drawing off resources, staff and funding.

But there is an alternative to centralised bureaucratic state services that does not have to be based on the pursuit of private profit. Steve Davies, writing in *Tribune* (20th February 2004), argues that allowing the oxygen of democracy to infuse public services is the way to modernise. Where the government has sought to decentralise public services into separate operations that can be commercialised and contracted out the accountants are happy but service users pay more and quality suffers. Davies argues that public services 'need flexibility, a capacity to adapt and respond to new demands that arise. Most of all they need to be accountable'. That means something else than the choice to rewrite the next contract.

So we have decentralised power in Scotland, Wales and London but enormous restrictions on the financial freedoms of these local bodies. When the Welsh Assembly sought to issue bonds as an alternative to PFI to finance capital expenditure the Westminster government blocked the move. Similarly, London Mayor Ken Livingstone and the Greater London Authority were stopped from taking a similar route to tube modernisation. The Hutton Report (chaired by Will Hutton of the Industrial Society) confirmed the approach desired by Livingstone and Transport for London supremo Bob Kiley was the most favourable approach. But all to no avail. The government dogmatically insisted both on Westminster control and the private finance of the modernisation programme.

More fundamentally public services reform must mean giving back to local government its powers. In 2004 Camden tenants voted no to an ALMO (Arms Length Management Organisation). In response, the government withheld millions of housing investment grant. A partial and tightly restricted 'public voice' such as that planned for the new foundation hospitals is not the answer.

An alternative would be the participatory budgetary system first introduced in the Brazilian city of Porto Alegre. This offers real choice to service users. Davies remarks that even the World Bank acknowledges this as an: 'innovative process of public investment and management...to mobilise citizen groups to take part in formulating the municipal budget'. Tens of thousands of citizens and social groups are involved in meetings and assemblies to discuss city budgets and priorities. In Britain, public services have been centralised, decentralised and commercialised but not democratised.

Contrast this experience with the producer co-operatives in parts of Spain, of Emilia Romagne or the sustained extended local democracy in the city of Bologna. Here democratic urban planning led to the preservation of the historic old town. A free fares policy was introduced during rush hours and free travel for the retired, young and unemployed. In the realm of consumer policy, health, education and social welfare the council pushed back the frontiers of bureaucratic control, experimenting with localised structures for user involvement. Municipal laundrettes combined with cultural innovations provided spaces for youth theatre, music and dance.

This takes us back to a future pioneered by the theoretician of democratic socialism, G.D.H. Cole. Cole was a champion of democratic, participatory, socialised state provision. He first outlined his ideas using the concept of guild socialism over ninety years ago. Although the concept now has a rather dated ring to it, in essence it was about producers, consumers and administrators collaboratively planning, developing and providing services and goods to society. In opposition to the Fabianism that has dominated Labour to this day Cole argues that we need to address issues both of methods of production, as well as distribution, which were and have been the focus of Fabians since the Webbs, and issues of democracy and accountability. His best biographer, Anthony Wright, now a Labour M.P., wrote in *G.D.H. Cole and Socialist Democracy* that he was 'the most democratic and radical of the British socialists'. This was reflected in his radical view of power that differed sharply from the collectivism of the left and right. In books like *The World of Labour*, *Guild Socialism Restated* and *Self Government in Industry*, written over a period from 1913 to the end of the First World War, Cole attempted to develop a coherent philosophy and strategy for a west European and British socialism. The enterprise involved a critique of Marxism, an attitude to Liberalism, a particular sociology and political economy, and a strong international perspective. He was a life-long member of the Labour Party, but to this day remains an outsider.

He started a classic Fabian embracing the Webbs' view of permeation and gradualness through parliament. The period of new militancy just before the war led by Irish, feminist and worker agitation wrought a change in Cole's thinking. Where he was inspired, particularly by the syndicalist movement and the creativity of the new militancy, Labour's leading figures hurried to denounce and refute what they depicted as a foreign challenge to parliamentarianism and orthodox Labour theory and practice. Ramsay MacDonald published *Syndicalism*, Philip Snowden *Socialism and Syndicalism* and the Webbs' *What Syndicalism Means*. (The former two leaders went on to become first Labour ministers then defectors to the 1931 National Government.) It all meant a threat to Fabian gradualist theory.

Cole argued that Fabianism had concentrated on problems of distribution to the neglect of the conditions of production. For him the primary problem was not poverty. This was but a symptom of slavery, the real disease. The slavery of the capitalist production system and the consequent dominance of bureaucracy over democracy in society. For Cole: 'So long as socialism remains mere bureaucratic monopoly it will be impotent'. Cole ditched Fabianism in 1913 but not the state itself, as Fabianism confused the present state with the state as it might and should become. In words of significant prescience, he saw this as a carelessness that would necessarily produce: 'merely a transference of authority from the capitalist to the bureaucrat' (*World of Labour*). But Cole was not an uncritical syndicalist proposing socialism through trade union action to abolish the state. He argued: 'the state is not through and through the capitalist dodge they are apt to represent it as being'. Cole did not see the state as irredeemably capitalist but at times 'had to act up to the standards of the community as a whole'.

This thinking also set him against Lenin's thesis in *State and Revolution* with its insistence on smashing the state. Cole argued for a policy of 'substitution' to be carried as far as possible before a direct and final clash with capitalism. Cole dissented from the communist position because of its refusal to recognise the primacy of preparation and training in the pursuit of power. The transition from capitalism to socialism was not as in Lenin (and Trotsky's) view one merely of strength in aggression, but also at least as much of 'fitness for administration'. This he dubbed the encroachment approach.

So the idea of transforming the state became a permanent feature of Cole's social thought, says Wright. Cole saw the state distorted by industrialism in general and by capitalism in particular. In a community environment, one where working people were in control through a multitude of groups, associations, local and national governments, control of the state would emerge in a purified form as an agency of expression for the organised will of the community. In contradistinction to classical Marxists the state in a socialist society would exercise functions that are not economic. This of course has become a marked feature of the state in post-modern capitalist society.

Cole championed devolution fifty years before it became popularised. For him the state was but one functional partner or elder brother to a range of devolved groups and association, not the father. In his model sovereignty was diffused throughout the whole complex of social arrangements. What was needed was the social machinery to embody this. Resting on his core pluralist principles were industrial self-government, community ownership and worker's control.

Unlike the Webbs, and many other Fabians, Cole was not seduced by Stalinism. He championed nationalisation with socialisation. He did not want the ship of the Labour Party coming round the 'Cape of state capitalism to the Sargossa Sea of State Socialism'. This would result in no change or worse and mean government would 'continue to repress all initiative, clog all endeavours and deny all freedom to the worker'. The Guild Socialists did not fancy living in that world and sought to transform every area of social activity, especially the workplace, into an arena of democracy. 'The aim was to prevent the loss of individuality and citizenship inherent in capitalism and state socialism.'

Cole's work can provide a rich filter bed for today's problems of modernising and transforming society. Cole was a great supporter of the first three years of the Attlee government, but by 1948 disillusion had set in. For him there had been a lamentable failure to explore socialisation, as opposed to nationalisation and a failure to engage in socialist education and propaganda to stimulate a popular demand 'for something more than a social service state'. For him, democratic socialism became stuck at welfarism on the one hand and mired in the Cold War anti-communism on the other.

How so little has changed in those fifty years. Although New Labour has sought to overcome the bureaucratic welfarist legacy of postwar Labour governments it has embraced an even more pernicious neo-liberal prospectus that can only end in tears. While on the international front 'Terrorism' and Weapons of Mass Destruction have replaced the Cold War as the modern day quicksand of Labour's failed internationalism.

As far as the modernisation of the public is concerned it is time to try a new model. The model would draw much inspiration from the work of Cole but seek to place his ideas in a twenty-first century environment. If Tony Blair really cares about what works he would look around the existing public sector. Many European municipalities have very successful services. Even in the U.S. state of California, Los Angeles (pre-Schwarzenegger) escaped the massive power cuts because power is provided by a municipal owned subsidiary. Ironically liberalisation and privatisation policies have allowed a partial re-nationalisation. The French state power company EdF now supplies electricity to London consumers. The Dutch government now runs the Merseyside suburban rail franchise and Danish state railways D.S.B. was short-listed for the integrated Kent franchise. Closer to home, in Education Services for example, if an L.E.A. is deemed by O.F.S.T.E.D. to be 'failing' why not use the expertise of another more effective L.E.A. rather than private corporations like Capita, C.E.A. or Nord Anglia. Instead, public services rich in talent, staff experience and public service ethos are being killed off. The cult of individualism, or 'personalisation', in Leadbetter's words, is gnawing away at the foundations of a collectivist, social spirit.

This is the theme of David Marquand's brilliant book *The Decline of the Public*. For Marquand the public is not just the public sector, the much-reduced nationalised industries and services but more widely public space and public spirit. Ironically, after twenty-five years of opprobrium and castigation Marquand sees a potential for a resurrection of the public. The very professionals held in such disregard by Tory and New Labour politicians – namely doctors, teachers, social workers and civil servants – now find their public esteem rising while that of the politicians has sunk to a low ebb.

The richness of Marquand's study is in its historical sweep. He traces the way that the 'public domain' was developed in Britain in the first place. The 'communal' and collective was very much part of the British tradition, not alien in the way Thatcher sought to portray it, and to some extent Blair does today. He nails the popular myth depicted in David Hare's play about railway privatisation *The Permanent Way*, that the 'public' is not in our D.N.A. He reminds us we invested in the railways and that was symptomatic of a strong tradition of British public endeavour. It is evident in the huge range of Victorian institutions from friendly societies, co-operatives and trade unions to sewage and water supply systems that set out to moderate the free market capitalism of early industrialisation. But for Marquand it was the rise of the professional that was central to the successful mainstreaming of the idea of public interest and enabled them to preside with authority over the growth of the welfare state in the middle decade of the last century.

However, the expansion of the public sector led to a commensurate growth and prosperity of professionals, particularly of town planners, lawyers, some doctors and nationalised industry managers. This in part led to their patronising claim to always 'know best'. This arrogance and lack of accountability gave us tower blocks without gardens, destroyed town centres, over-sized comprehensive schools, a huge bureaucracy which would have been less unacceptable had it not been so unaccountable. When Thatcher set about selling off the 'family silver' she found a quiescent and disaffected public relatively indifferent to marketization with its principles of competition and efficiency.

To his credit Blair started to reverse the state centralisation process and reform the public but has adopted the tools of the right to do so: authoritarianism, re-imposing central control, commercialisation, and silencing debate where discussion and democracy have to be centre stage. New Labour sees much apathy. But civic engagement, whether it be by pensioners, protesters against the Iraq war or environmentalists and anti-globalisation demonstrators is on the increase.

In June 2003, The Labour Party affiliated Fabian Society published a pamphlet by Home Office Minister Hazel Blears, proposing to turn key parts of the public sector into mutual organisations owned and controlled by local people and their users. Voters would be given direct power over the financing and management of public services such as schools, libraries, health centres, hospitals and parks along the lines being followed in foundation hospitals. Home Secretary David Blunkett has also announced similar plans for the criminal justice system with directly elected police boards. Blears argues: 'Without creating a tangible connection between citizens and their public services beyond narrow concepts of consultation and participation, the process of alienation and disengagement from mainstream politics and institutions will continue'. It is time to take power from the politicians, bureaucrats, experts and officials it will have to amount to more than the model proposed for foundation hospitals where selected local people get to vote occasionally on issues of management and planning. Elections of members of stakeholder boards and non-executive directors would be a start.

But little has been heard since the pamphlet's launch at Number

Ten. It has sunk into the authoritarian populist mire into which the whole government is sinking. Rather than introducing market forces the far more powerful force of users and stakeholders could help breathe reforming oxygen in our public services. Encouraging and facilitating widespread democratic participation could help reinvigorate Britain's flagging democratic system. It's not postal voting in supermarkets or online voting that will revive interest in politics (although turnout in May 2005 would have been lower than sixty-one per cent without these changes) but a reinvigoration of participatory democracy in the workplace, community, schools, health and other public services. Cole, along with Rousseau and J.S. Mill recognised that we learn to participate, to take control, by participating and feelings of political efficacy are more likely to be developed in a participatory environment. Carole Pateman in *Participation and Democratic Theory* argues that: 'evidence of a participatory authority structure might also be effective in diminishing tendencies towards non-democratic attitudes in the individual'. This is precisely the opposite of the possessive individualism currently corroding the collective and social ethic.

Active citizenship education is schools involving the empowering of student councils; the involvement of school students in a wider range of decision-making from teacher appointments to curriculum and teaching reviews could nurture a positive education for democracy. The emphasis must be on participation rather than consultation with the school community given a real voice in the shaping and direction of school policy along the Scandinavian model. If the government really wants to empower schools they should be funding school student unions and organisers rather than pursuing the divisive and spurious proposals for school independence contained in the latest Education White Paper.

If we are seeking to create a deeper-rooted democracy and more empowered citizenry where better to start than with young people and working class people. Why not have school students with voting powers on governing bodies? And why not have workers with voting and scrutiny powers on boards of directors? And why not further empower elected local councils to decide with users key questions of education and children's services, housing, environment, policing and transport? These are elementary measures that could help restore confidence in public services and greater levels of involvement in civic life. Even with the limited powers invested in the London Mayor, Ken Livingstone has demonstrated how to be popular, radical and innovative without cow-towing to private capital and the market.

Elected local and London government, the Welsh Assembly and

Scottish parliament have demonstrated how neighbourhood accountability can produce progressive outcomes. It is time central government stopped centralising, let go and opened the pores of participatory democracy in civil society.

Subscribe to *Chartist*

Chartist is read by those on the left who want politics beyond slogans and easy answers. Why not join the growing body of supporter subscribers which enables you to attend readers' meetings and the AGM. Alternatively, just take out an ordinary subscription for a year.

Chartist also needs sellers. If you want to help promote a new socialism fill in the form below.

❏ I enclose £15 for an ordinary subscription, starting from the next issue

❏ I want_____ copies of *Chartist* to sell

❏ I enclose £30/15 waged/unwaged for a supporter's subscription, starting from number

❏ I enclose £25 for an institutional subscription (£35 overseas).

❏ I enclose £35/20 for an overseas supporters/ordinary subscription

❏ I enclose a donation of _____

Name _____
Address _____
_____**Postcode** _____
Phone _____ **E-Mail** _____

Please send to Chartist Publications, PO Box 52751, LONDON EC2P 2XF

Or subscribe online at www.chartist.org.uk

Sweet harmony:

Integration and the multi-cultural society are not incompatible

Anna Bluston

The issue of individual and collective culture and identity has always been a difficult and contentious topic – never more so than today with the debate reignited by the July 2005 London bombings and the ongoing 'War on Terror' hardening British, as well as global, attitudes into an 'us and them' mentality.

The concept of integration is at the heart of any discussion in creating communities and a society. It is important to state what this means, and to distinguish it from assimilation – a dangerous concept – and one which many societies, such as France, believe will enable a stable society when in fact, as recent events have shown, the opposite is true.

Assimilation follows the 'melting pot' idea: that people will come from all different places and fully embrace the culture they have moved to, giving up their own identity and being the same as the majority culture. Many societies believe that only by assimilation will there be a stable society; that immigrants need to learn to fit in with the majority and adopt their customs, thus maintaining a national identity. I believe this is fatal, and by denying difference and repressing individuality resentment is stored up to explode later in a violent manner, as the 2005 French riots so clearly demonstrated.

Integration, conversely, entails a true celebration of multiculturalism, so that individuals and groups feel part of a British identity and share common values while at the same time retaining and celebrating their own cultural and individual distinctiveness. This approach, which, admittedly, is a difficult balance between individual rights and collective responsibility is the only way to create a harmonious, fulfilled, cohesive society.

These issues are also related to the ideas of 'tolerance' and 'pluralism'. Tolerance is connected to tolerating, which means that you put up with ideas, situations and people that you don't like or agree with, but sweep the problems under the carpet to maintain superficial harmony. On the contrary, pluralism is about celebrating difference, and genuinely accepting others for who and what they are.

This article attempts to address the problems involved in creating the latter ideal, and to find solutions to enable Britain to become such an integrated society with values of respect for and acceptance of others. While it is up to individuals themselves to try to be responsible citizens, and for community leaders to educate their communities about integration and build links with the wider society, there is also a lot that the government can do to help integration.

One key issue in this debate is faith schools. The current government is devoted to vastly increasing the number of religious schools, mainly or wholly for children who are born into families of one particular religion, or branch of a religion. The argument in favour of such schools is that they often have 'better' values than secular schools, as almost all religions have at the heart of their teaching respect and love for others – charity, caring, and decency – and will therefore be able to pass on these values to the children in their care, helping to promote these ideals in the wider society.

While anyone has the right to believe in whatever they choose and be able to express their beliefs, faith schools in fact end up causing divisions in society and promote the opposite values that is the core of the religious teaching. They promote divisiveness, segregation, and ghettoisation, with their pupils only used to mixing with those from the same religious or even cultural background, which can only cause more intolerance and prejudice in the wider society. I fully support and believe in the value of religious education: all schools should be fully comprehensive and inclusive, across ethnic, religious, cultural and class divides, teaching a broad and varied religious education curriculum. If people wish to go to extra-curricula classes, run by their own faith groups, out of school hours, then they should have the right to do so, as with any other specialist activity. But school should be a place where as wide a curriculum is studied as possible, with as wide a variety of pupils, to promote and encourage broad-minded, well rounded individuals.

Having said that school is not the place to promote one particular religious point of view, I would still fully endorse the right of individuals to express their religious affiliations in school, such as Muslim girls being allowed to wear hijab. France has banned this right to freedom of expression in an attempt to heal religious and racial divisions, therefore making everyone the same. It has been demonstrated that the opposite is true, and this prejudiced and oppressive law has simply served to alienate French Muslims from French society, causing them to harbour bitterness and resentment towards their state.

The key point here is the difference between the 'promotion' of religion as opposed to freedom of expression. Wearing hijab, a crucifix or kippah (Jewish skull cap) is not proselytising. This issue instead cuts to the heart of the integration versus assimilation message. Any individual, whether religious, secular, or part of any subculture, should have the right to express their affiliation to their group and feel that they are embraced by mainstream society with the right to express and share their beliefs but not dominate others. To deny this human right of freedom of expression causes more divisions in society and alienation, which is the root cause of tensions and civil unrest between different groups.

Another main point central to achieving social unity is a healthy sense of national identity. Taking pride in one's country and celebrating its sporting achievements, for example, is a way for people to show pride in the country they live in, either from birth or by choice, and does not exclude their right to support other countries or have other identities as well. This includes all citizens, whatever their colour or ethnic background, particularly the many second and third-generation immigrants, who feel as much English as anything else. Uniting people under this common banner of 'Englishness' does much good for race relations and feelings of identity. Of course, there will always be hooligans who take the concept too far, especially in football unfortunately, but this minority must not be allowed to spoil it for the rest of us.

There is no reason why people should not be allowed to feel allegiance to several identities. Norman (Lord) Tebbit's famous 'cricket test' is misguided. There is no reason why people can't support several teams, and if those are competing, be able to choose their sporting allegiance without feeling a traitor for abandoning one of them. Whichever sporting team people support, sharing common values of tolerance, respect, understanding and a sense of unity with others are far more crucial to a social cohesion than which side you support in a cricket match.

Although multi-culturalism, diversity and pluralism are to be welcomed and embraced, to form any cohesive society there needs to be a set of basic values that everyone adheres to create a safe, harmonious environment and to ensure true integration. The basic requirements for everyone, for example, are that all citizens should speak the native language and therefore all immigrants wishing to live here should learn English. They also must agree to obey the rule of law, and not endanger the life of anyone in the nation. Citizenship classes for schoolchildren should be fully supported, as should much more teaching about Britain's history, politics, and democracy and the structure of government. The introduction of 'citizenship tests' for those wishing to become British Citizens has been much derided, but this is a valuable and useful idea, and will aid integration if the questions are carefully considered, focussing on Britain's laws, history, and cultural traditions. Everyone, from whatever cultural background, should feel proud to share a sense of English, or British identity, and still be able to hold several other identities comfortably, not feeling a sense of conflict between them. Many have successfully managed to integrate: second and third-generation immigrants wear their traditional clothes at home and speak their parents' native language, at the same time fully participating in traditional British customs and having friends from all different backgrounds. This is to be welcomed and encouraged, and there is no need for English, or any other form of cultural expression, to be valued more highly than another.

The problem seems to come from several sides when pressures come from different communities about choosing one sort of culture over another. This is not only a case of religious or ethnic minority communities. Although society seems to be much more liberal and accepting of diversity than in previous times, there is still an enormous pressure to conform to a stereotype of one specific type of person. I often get asked by nine year-olds if I am a 'goth' or a 'grunger', because I often wear black or have black nail polish. I tell them not to label people, and that I wear different things at different times. I remember being in school when there would be fights in a local park between 'ravers' and 'metalers' – people who liked different types of music would literally try to kill each other because their preferred type of music so defined them. It formed so much of the core of their identity that they could not tolerate people who they felt opposed their values just because they listened to a different type of music.

These examples demonstrate that it is not only 'immigrants' who are seen as 'the other' and felt to be separate or excluded: many different subcultures feel only an identity with their own particular group and unable to accept or tolerate difference.

Multi-culturalism means integration, and should involve different groups of people learning from each other and sharing ideas, without losing their own sense of identity. For example, instead of a strict divide of opposing cultures between 'religious' and 'secular', both groups would do extremely well to learn from each other if they adopted some of the better principles and values that each side has to offer. There are many current religious practices, observed stringently by millions, which appear outdated, anachronistic, even discriminatory in modern societies. It is right that such customs are held up to scrutiny, even criticism, by wider society, and evaluated as to their worth and value. The argument that something is part of someone's 'culture' is no justification to break the law, persecute people, or deny anyone their human rights. By being exposed to modernity, many cultures can learn possibly more 'liberal' ideas.

Equally, secular society has much to learn from the religious and religious values. All religions have at their core the values of love, respect, justice and mercy and consider 'the bigger picture'. Our current secular society would do much to learn from these, with its values of greed, materialism, selfishness, and short-term thinking, which many religious followers condemn, and try to bring 'holy' values to this world. They are also right to do so. People from all different backgrounds of religion, culture, and beliefs have much to learn from each other, and in an integrated, multicultural society, the sharing of ideas, full discussion, and the critique of any and every sincerely-held value system would aid democracy, tolerance, understanding, harmony, and maybe even necessary change.

In conclusion, the concept of identity is highly complex, and creating social cohesion with so many diverse groups and individuals is a task that needs commitment from everyone involved – government and citizens – and uniting people under a common British identity and allegiance needs to be carefully balanced with encouraging and promoting diversity and celebrating difference. This is essential to the well-being of the nation and to create happy citizens and a healthy society.

What is *Chartist*?

Chartist is the voice of the thinking Left. *Chartist* is a bi-monthly magazine written and read by those on the Left who want politics beyond slogans and banal clichés.

The editorial policy of *Chartist* is to promote debate amongst people active in radical politics about the contemporary relevance of democratic socialism across the spectrum of politics, economics, science, philosophy, art, interpersonal relations – in short, the whole realm of social life.

Our concern is with both democracy and socialism. The history of last century has made it abundantly clear that the mass of the population of the advanced capitalist countries will have no interest in any form of socialism which is not thoroughly democratic in its principles, its practices, its morality and its ideals. Yet the consequences of this deep attachment to democracy – one of the great advances of our epoch are seldom reflected in the discussions and debates amongst active socialists.

Chartist is not a party publication. It brings together people who are interested in socialism, some of whom are active in the Labour Party and the trade union movement. It is concerned to deepen and extend a dialogue with all other socialists, and with activists from other movements involved in the struggle to find democratic alternatives to the oppression, exploitation and injustices of capitalism and class society.

Chartist welcomes articles, of up to 1,500 words, and letters from all its readers.

For more information on contributing email editor@chartist.org.uk

To read some of the best articles from the latest *Chartist,* go to our website: www.chartist.org.uk

Bread first, then poetry:

Or why socialism must remain anchored in reality

Don Flynn

"Amongst the highly placed
It is considered low to talk about food
The fact is: they have
Already eaten"
Bertolt Brecht: From a German War Primer

The dismal science of political economy chaffs and restrains the most creative spirits – even those who are its practitioners. If the nineteenth century pioneers of modern political systems felt obliged to pay economics any attention, it was usually in order that they might plot an escape route from out of its abysmal grip.

This was as true for Marx as it was for then more influential contemporaries of the ilk of Disraeli and Gladstone. The architect of scientific socialism spent decades deconstructing the logic of Smith and Ricardo in the hope that beyond the boundaries of their undoubted insights there might lay the realm of eventual human freedom.

And so for a century after the publication of the *Communist Manifesto*, the basic stance of socialism was unquestionably materialist. Understanding the reasons why poverty was created in society was the fundamental task of every socialist, whether Marxian or social democratic in orientation.

Yet another aspect of the revolution in thinking wrought by the acolytes of New Labourism has been to bring to an end the powerful sense at the heart of the traditional labour and socialist movement that and understanding and critique of the nature of contemporary capitalism is the starting point for its political mission. It achieved this breakthrough by simply abandoning the idea capitalism was a categorical imperative of the modern world in order to look instead as the supposedly boundary-less flow of intermingling processes which swept the economic into the social and political, and probably mixed in a bit of the artistic on the way.

This was a step that had been urged upon modern politicians by the great and influential liberal philosopher, Karl Popper in his charge against 'essentialism' as one of the fundamental evils of the epoch. Essentialism is what happened when thinkers assumed a discreet entity being formed from their own work of critical analysis, and then pursuing this beast in the real world as though it actually existed. In doing this they elided over the real conditions of human existence, favouring instead their own ideal versions.

The path from materialism to New Labour's version of liberalism has not been marked by cataclysmic rupture. Rather the drift from economics to sociology as the underpinning rationale for its work was aided by the transitional period of revisionist economics that emerged after World War Two. Exemplified by the thinking of Tony Crosland, though in fact built on the work of a previous generation of social democrats which included the likes of Evan Durbin, Douglas Jay, et al, the insight here was not that capitalism had ceased to be an important category of thought for socialist analysis, but that it had been transformed in the middle decades of the twentieth century into a different type of thing altogether.

Thinking in terms which made a dialogue with orthodox Marxists at least possible (indeed, their earliest progenitors, such as the German social democrat Eduard Bernstein, had been orthodox Marxists) the revisionists purported that socialist strategy now had to be re-orientated around the fact that capitalism had now transcended the limitations of a system based rooted in private ownership of the productive means, had overcome its tendencies towards turbulence and periodic crisis, and was now capable of being socialised by rooting its operations in strategic economic planning, the redistributive effects of the welfare state, and the perfection of political democracy within the nation state. The 'future of socialism' Crosland wrote in his book of that title, was for a social-democratic Labour government to work with this process to produce a stable social system expressing the ultimate value of equality between citizens.

Political economy did not cease to be relevant to this generation of thinkers, but in breaking with the Marxian prediction of perpetual crisis overwhelming the system, they crafted a strategy in which technocrats could assume the initiative and plan for the ordered running of the capitalist system and the rational distribution of its goods and services.

For some in the Labour Party, this perspective, remarkably successful for a lengthy period across the 1950s and 1960s, was fundamentally challenged by the crisis which emerged in the 1970s (for more, see the following article), and which suggested that the old instabilities of the system had reappeared.

But the social-democrats were not prepared to concede the argument this easily. Wilson and Callaghan readily adapted to the dominant analysis of the reasons for the new problems – that 'big government' was sustaining itself by printing too much money and thereby destabilising the system by stoking up inflation – and came up with the first versions of monetarism as the means to tackle these developments. Its consequence was to provoke a major crisis in the social-democratic left, overturning the consensus achieved by agreement on the importance of economic planning and the operations of the welfare state, and splitting the movement into deeply antagonistic right and left wings.

Enter Margaret Thatcher as the beneficiary of these divisions, and the true heir to the monetarist policies pioneered by Labour's right wing. Unhampered by the social conscience of ethical socialism, Thatcher took the policy where it logically led – the crashing of the manufacturing base of British capitalism, which had depended on the infrastructure of economic planning for its functioning, and rolling back the welfare state and the public sector through budget cut-backs and privatisation.

The failure of either wing of the Labour Party to come up with a strategy to challenge Thatcherism meant that the experiment with right-wing economic policies was allowed to run its disastrous course, with devastating consequences for the post-war system of governance.

Despite, rather than because of Thatcherite policies, the steep decline of the British economy was arrested near the point of rock bottom when new scales of economy were achieved by radically restructured enterprises, and the whole process of accumulation could begin again.

The Labour Party's political fortunes followed a similar trajectory. At the point of the first signs of recovery in the economy it pieced together a supposed critique of the Thatcher and Major years, which essentially conceded the most important arguments to right-wing political economists, but opened up space for a quibble over the details of their policies. Tory insensitivity to the nuances of economic developments, they said, had meant that recovery had been by way of a jerky 'boom-bust' cycle which greater astuteness would have avoided. And it was on precisely its claim for its own competence in such matters that a New Labour economic strategy was launched.

Ironically, it was at precisely this point, and despite the evidence that instability was reasserting itself as a fundamental feature of the way the whole world was now running its economic affairs, that New Labour chose to abolish the category of political economy altogether, and to offer as its replacement the prospect of technocratic 'prudence'.

After all, this is a government which proclaims its single most important reform in the running of economic affairs as the giving up of its residual authority to set interest rates – i.e. to influence the growth or retraction of demand in the economy – to the non-politicians of the Bank of England. With no big ambitions left for establishing the overall shape of a British economy, and the purposes for which it was run, policy subsided into a permanent schmoozing of celebrity corporate chiefs in the hope that an association with their apparent success might transmit into a feeling on the part of the public that the government was also at least semi-competent, and the rather clever dreaming up of new, discrete tax wheezes to pay the bills of obvious, much needed investment in infrastructure.

When all you want to do in the way of economic policy is to plod on quietly and pay the bills the last thing you want to be told is that all the things that had established the boundaries of your secure little world were becoming unhinged. Amongst the looming problems was the fact that the permanent growth of markets, assumed to have been secured by privatisation and globalisation, was revealing hitherto unsuspected instabilities based on the failing credit-worthiness of the one big national economy capable of barging the rest of the world into acceptance of universalised neo-con economic policies. Even the in the most neat and prim households, the crockery tends to fall out of the cupboards and onto the floor during Richter scale-five earth tremors.

The character of the fundamental flaws in the structure of the globalised economy is explored in greater details in the chapter by Frank Lee, which follows. The argument being pursued here, however, is not just the simple fact that New Labour has got the political economy of modern capitalism wrong, but that because of the very structure of its most fundamental thinking, it is has immense difficulties in understanding the character of capitalism as an economic system at all.

Others have written about the sociological bias of New Labour's thought, and its understanding of modern society as a fusion of social and cultural phenomena in ways which extinguish the distinct realms of the social, political, economic and cultural. The onrush of modernity itself, destroying tradition and imposing on individuals the obligation to understand their predicament as an entirely new chapter in the condition of human life, means that everything has to be understood from the standpoint of the 'modern', rather than the social, or the political, or the economic. Whilst there is still meaning to be attached to these words and concepts, it is subordinate to the biggest meaning of them all; the almost religious sense 'that all that is solid melts into air.'

It is ironic that it is quote from Marx and Engels' *Communist Manifesto*, describing the consequences of the ascendancy of the bourgeoisie during an earlier globalising phase of capitalism, is now so frequently used to describe the claimed insights of New Labour. Where for Marx and Engels it marked the beginning of scrutiny of the record and the role of the nascent commercial classes, for New Labour thinkers it is the stage at which we can assume that their work is done, and all that remains for politicians is to persuade the masses to accommodate themselves to the new reality which has been created. This means accepting the permanency of the categories of bourgeois social thinking (that society can be maintained functionally, to deliver to commerce and what is left of industry the things it needs, just as commerce and industry functions to deliver profit to its shareholders); bourgeois political thinking (that politics has in fact ceased to be politics in the sense of marking out the terrain in which conflicting social interests engage, but has become a branch of apolitical administration); and of bourgeois economics (that resources will be unproblematically allocated by the laws of supply and demand to the places where they can be guaranteed to maximise opportunities for profit).

For New Labour all issues of governance and administration are essentially technical and, despite the stubbornness of people in their slow acceptance of the absence of an alternative, uncontroversial. Sooner or later the political parties will converge on acceptance of this point and all that will remain of politics at that point will be the sort of factional quibbling and argument that you will hear round the fringes of any boardroom, as the representatives of the leading shareholders dispute amongst themselves the meaning of the latest company financial reports for their returns of their investment.

So much of this viewpoint depends for its credibility on the view that they way we run industry and commerce is not a fitting subject for political argument, because there is nothing fundamentally wrong with the way the system is managed. All that matters nowadays is a central government being canny enough to recognise in advance the hiccups which the system will always be prone to produce, in the way of inadequate management producing lower productivity or imbalances between core enterprise activity and the availability of appropriate infrastructure. No ideology is required to produce solutions to these problems when they do arise, and any solution merely has to show that it 'works' in order to be judged good enough. 'What works' is perhaps the chief mantra of New Labourism, seeking to reduce all policy discussion to the narrow objective of producing an outcome that can be reported well in the media headlines.

The high hopes of New Labourism will be dashed by nothing less important than palpable demonstration that the interests bound up in the running of a capitalist economy do not smoothly mesh with the need for social cohesion and good administration, but in fact threaten society with the danger, more severe in some periods that in others, of vast dislocation at times when the market reveals that it has a logic of its own which is not amenable to socialisation. Political radicals have sketched out the areas in which it is obvious, to them at least, that this has been happening during periods when even rapid economic growth has obscured the amount of misery and poverty which exists in society. Damage to the environment, now understood to be potentially cataclysmic in the short span of the next fifty years or so; the failure to produce a democratic world politics at the rate in which world economics has become ascendant; and the savage inequalities of wealth across the planet, demonstrate the fact that even during the good years capitalism throws up problems which, over time, it might become beyond the capacity of society to solve.

But few think that the years immediately ahead will provide the good times which New Labour desperately needs to support its case that all can be entrusted to men and women of good will and sufficient talent to battle through to solve the problems. Turbulence is growing across the system and the worries of the world's bankers mount as a global credit system of Byzantine complexity threatens to implode.

The chapter that follows sets out the analysis which suggests that turbulence will grow to 'tsunami' proportions. When that happens what is left of New Labour, with its feeble dreams of life in a society which has transcended politics and economics, will be finally washed away.

If democratic socialism is not to be washed away with it, it will be because it has asserted an understanding of the contemporary nature of capitalism against the 'feel-good' cheerleaders who currently dominate the mainstream of politics. Its political programme will be immensely strengthened in the meantime if the politics of the left re-appropriate the area where the practitioners of the dismissal science now hold sway, and discovers the ways in which the making of bread can also be the way to make poetry, and civilisation itself, anew.

On the cusp:

Is a new global economic order inevitable?

Frank Lee

'There is no means of avoiding the final collapse of a boom brought about by credit expansion. The alternative is only whether the crisis should come sooner as the result of voluntary abandonment of further credit expansion, or later as a final and total catastrophe of the currency involved.' (Von Mises, L., Human Action - A Treatise on Economics, 1949, quoted in Duncan, R., The Dollar Crisis, 2003)

'The ultimate reason for all real crises always remains the poverty and restricted consumption of the masses as opposed to the drive of capitalist production to develop the productive forces as though only the absolute consuming power of society constituted their limit.' (Marx, K., Das Kapital volume 3 p.484)

The Background:

The capitalist system is an historical phenomenon whose characteristics may be listed as follows:

1. Private property in the means of production.
2. A system of generalised commodity production.
3. The relentless conversion of all existing use-values into exchange-values.
4. The evolution of money, not merely as a store of value and means of circulation, but entailing a separate sphere of finance and speculation.
5. The growth of the system beyond national boundaries into a global system, involving the development of trade, imperialism and

globalisation.
6. An expanding system of accumulation and growth.
7. The application of science and technology to the process of production in order to effect this ongoing accumulation.
8. The extraction of surplus value to be realised as money profit through sale on a market.
9. The continual expansion of the market in order to realise this ever increasing and expanding surplus value.
10. The transition from the free-market into monopolistic/oligopolistic market structures with a system of administered prices and wages.
11. A specific set of social relations of production reflected in culture and legal/political frameworks.
12. Boom and bust. Capitalism moves in cycles varying from the relatively mild, to wild and febrile expansion followed by calamitous collapse. These cycles are short, medium and long term, variously termed the business cycle, Kuznets cycles, Kondtratiev long-waves, and long centuries. They take place concurrently. Crises are inherent in the capitalist system; they are the primary mechanism whereby, having reached a stage of stagnation, the system is able to restructure itself and continue the process of accumulation at a higher level.

The evolution of the capitalist system can be traced back to Italy in the fifteenth century, notably the city-states of Venice and Genoa. Looking at the development of capitalism during the course of the twentieth (i.e. American) century it is possible to identify a number of distinct phases. Firstly the belle époque of capitalist civilization which lasted up until the First World War. Secondly the post-war situation of generalised instability: heavy and cyclical unemployment combined with stock market booms and feverish expansion - the roaring twenties. This period culminated in the Wall Street crash in 1929, followed by the great depression. At this stage many, if not most, commentators did not believe that capitalism could survive this cataclysm of depression followed by war. Even the system's most ardent partisans, such as Joseph A Schumpeter, were pronouncing the last rites: 'Can capitalism survive? No I do not think that it can.' (*Capitalism, Socialism and Democracy*, 1943).

It came as something as a surprise therefore that post-war capitalism should have the most successful run in its history. The period from the late 1940s till the early 1970s represented the 'golden age' of capitalism. All the technological spin-offs from wartime production were now applied to civilian use with the corollary of enormously enhanced productivity. Moreover all the pent-up demand held in check by wartime rationing and austerity was released, providing an expanding market for the flood of commodities coming out of the factories. It is important to bear in mind that the collectivist ethos of the war was carried over into the peace, so that economic growth was evenly distributed among the population as a whole. During this period therefore the whole of society prospered. However, this was not to last.

'Over the period 1947-1973 the incomes of all groups rose roughly at the same rapid clip, more than 2.5% annually. That is to say the good years were about as equally good for everyone. Between 1973 and 1979, as the economy was battered by slow productivity growth and oil shocks, income growth became much slower and more uneven. Finally, after 1979, a new pattern emerged: generally slower income growth, but in particular a strong tilt in the growth pattern, with incomes rising much faster at the top end of the distribution hierarchy, than in the middle, and actually declining at the bottom.' (Krugman, P., *Peddling Prosperity*,1994)

Thus we had arrived at the latest phase of capitalism - the leaden age. Viewed historically this change should not perhaps really come as any surprise. The movement of society away from the collectivist wartime and post-war model was really nothing more than a reversion to type. The whole period from 1940 until 1973 may be regarded as an historical aberration: a period where capitalist interests were on the defensive, faced with a very combative coalition of political forces demanding change. However when the post-war boom began to run out of steam the ancien regime saw its chance to re-impose its rule, and it did so with ruthless intent.

'And what rough beast, its hour come round at last
Slouches toward Bethlehem to be born'
(W.B. Yeats *The Second Coming*)

Phase I - Neo-liberalism Triumphant

The counter-revolutionary wave that began in the late 1970s was to surge on into the new century. Now underlying all of the practises of government policy was the simple notion that control of the money supply and the sacred trinity of privatisation-deregulation-liberalisation were all that was needed to restore dynamism to a capitalist system undermined by excessive rules, regulations and red-tape (though the former policy was to be discarded).

Globalisation represented the projection of these policy prescriptions to an international level. Trite? Simplistic? Certainly. But hey, who says ideology has to be logically consistent? As the theologian

Turtellian once remarked about the existence of God: 'It is to be believed because it is absurd.' In policy terms this comprised of privatisation of publicly-owned industries, sale of council houses, breaking the power of the unions through legal and other means, such as mass unemployment, tendering and outsourcing, the creation of 'flexible' labour markets, de-industrialization, and the encouragement of inward investment. These policies formed the core of the new order. At the international level exchange controls, which had placed restrictions on the inflow and outflow of capital, were removed. Companies could also now re-locate to low-cost venues if and when it suited them. The era of 'globalisation' had arrived.

Globalisation, that is, the increasing integration and inter-dependence of national economies, along with the concomitant erosion of the national sovereignty of nation states, has been characterised by the increasing movement of goods, services, capital, ideas and people across national borders; the development of regional trading blocs; and the growth in the number and reach of global corporations. This process was driven forward by decisions taken by governments and by un-elected, unaccountable multilateral organisations such as the World Trade Organisation (W.T.O.) through its various rounds of trade liberalisation. Such policies facilitating the globalisation process did not happen fortuitously: they were the outcome of an ideological agenda and active political choices. The fact is that the whole project of global economic integration has been politically driven.

It should also be borne in mind, however, that the extent of globalization is somewhat exaggerated. Economics operates at three levels. In order of importance these are:

1. The local (or national).
2. The regional (E.U., N.A.F.T.A. etc.).
3. The global.

Something like three-quarters of economic activity - in terms of both production and consumption - is locally based; this is particularly true of the service sector. Secondly, up to eighty per cent of trade and investment flows (direct and portfolio) are between the so-called Triad of N.A.F.T.A., the E.U. and Japan and now China together with the newly industrialised economies of the Far East (N.I.C.S. – South Korea, Taiwan, Singapore and Hong Kong). 'Triadization' may therefore be a more apposite term than globalisation in this context. For purposes of clarification it is worth pursuing the point further. Globalisation is basically a hypothesis based upon some extremely dubious premises: discrete national economies have ceased to exist having been subsumed into an international system by global processes and transactions. Transnational corporations have become de-nationalised. Staffed with a cosmopolitan management, the strategy and reach of these new T.N.Cs are global rather than national. National governments can no longer regulate or control these T.N.Cs and the international global system becomes autonomous; now control can only be effected at the international level.

This is clearly not the case. What seems to be taking place is hardly a new phenomenon (see Hirst and Thompson 1996). In this scenario the principal economic units - banks, corporations, etc. - remain national, although international aspects of the economy, for example trade, foreign direct investment (F.D.I.) and Multinational Corporations (M.N.Cs) are assuming increasing importance. M.N.Cs obviously retain a substantive national H.Q. and production base that contains most of their market as well as being the centre of these same companies' higher managerial and technological functions. Global strategy, organisational auditing investment and finance, as well as higher-level research and development (R&D), marketing strategies and design will be carried out at these H.Qs. Being primarily national, therefore, M.N.Cs are amenable to political control by the mother country. If such companies are increasingly able to do as they please - tax avoidance for example - it is only with the connivance of the nation state. Moreover, states still remain in charge of essential prerogatives that are the basis of their national sovereignty. No supranational authority has yet been designed to replace this system of national government. If the globalization thesis holds anywhere then it is at the level of international finance. But even here governments could, if they wanted to badly enough and if they acted at least at a regional level, call the bluff of the moneymen. The extent that moneyed interests get away with murder is in exact proportion to the lack of political will on the side of elected governments. 'The growth of tax havens and bank regulation havens could easily have been checked at an early stage. The home governments of these banks, corporations and insurance companies which took advantage of them could at any time have put them out of bounds.' (Strange, S., *Casino Capitalism*, 1987) Governments - at least those that counted - not only did nothing to check the runaway tendencies of de-regulated global capitalism, they actually encouraged these same tendencies.

The 1980s and the roaring 1990s represented the apogee of the new order. Yuppies, surging stock markets, fabulous fortunes being made, and, above all, the absolute dominance of international finance. Later capitalism is dominated by finance capital. Indeed, ninety to ninety-five per cent of money circulating around the globe is not connected with trade purposes or productive investment, but is merely speculative, or hot money, looking to make a quick profit in the equity, property, forex and derivatives markets.

Credit, Booms and Bubbles

The problem (although at that time it was not perceived as such) was that the collapse of the Bretton Woods system – where the de facto dollar dominance was backed by gold – had been replaced by a pure dollar standard. This meant that the United States could simply print dollars to cover its trade imbalances, and since the dollar was the international reserve currency then the rest of the world would have to lump it. However, this would, if carried out in perpetuity, have inflationary as well as other deadly consequences, but the temptation for the U.S. was too great. Thus emerged the Eurodollar market; a mass of U.S. dollars circulating outside the U.S. considerably larger than those dollars in domestic circulation, together with the growth in dollar denominated assets – viz., U.S. Treasury Bills, equities (as quoted on the Dow Jones Industrial Average and high-tech market like N.A.S.D.A.Q), U.S. government agency securities, U.S. Corporate Bonds, F.D.I. into the U.S. and others. The key currency afforded to the dollar meant that the U.S. was able to enjoy a standard of living that the productivity of its economy did not merit. During the three decades since the collapse of the Bretton Woods system the U.S. has incurred a cumulative current account deficit of more the U.S$3 trillion. The U.S. is able to consume the rest of the world's goods by the issue of a mountain of I.O.Us at low rates of interest and of extremely dubious value.

The structural problem is that the U.S. economy consumes too much, saves too little, and is uncompetitive on world markets. This has resulted in chronic trade imbalances and a need to finance the voracious American consumer by tapping into the world's savings and trade surpluses. In 2003 the U.S.'s net liabilities to the rest of the world represented around twenty-five per cent of its G.D.P. and it absorbed some seventy per cent of the world's savings through various forms of investment. This dollar gap is covered by the issue of Eurodollars and other dollar denominated assets. However, such policies cannot be kept in place in perpetuity since it is unlikely that the U.S. will be able to service relentlessly growing and crippling debts. Water cannot be turned into wine. Countries which live beyond their means - even those endowed with the global reserve currency - must of necessity eventually devalue.

The current dollar glut also demonstrated the interconnected nature of the global monetary crisis: this was instanced in the collapse of the Japanese bubble in 1989. Japan, then (and still) the world's foremost creditor nation had been running massive trade surpluses with the U.S. Why should a dollar surplus nation run into problems of this kind?

'When more money enters a country than leaves it, that money, (unless it is hidden in a mattress or destroyed) is almost always deposited in that countries banking system...it then sparks off a process of credit creation unless the central bank takes action to sterilise the capital inflows. When the sums of money entering the country are very large, and when the monetary authorities fail to absorb that inflow by issuing a sufficient amount of bonds to soak up the additional liquidity, the outcome is a rapid expansion of the money supply and the emergence of an economic bubble. That is what occurred in Japan.' (Duncan, R., Op.cit.)

When money supply expanded rapidly inflation was experienced not as consumer price inflation but as asset price inflation (i.e. steep price rises in assets such as property, shares, commodities such as precious metals and oil). The Nikkei surged to over 40,000, property prices boomed, the exchange rate of the Yen rocketed. From excess credit, to boom, to bubble and finally to bust followed by credit crunch and slump, Japan had to live with the consequences for the next fifteen years: monetary policy had been exhausted, interest rates reduced to zero. Additional attempts by the government at traditional Keynesian pump-priming had also initially failed to bear fruit. Government debt went up to one hundred and forty per cent of G.D.P. These events led Japan to be downgraded to almost basket-case status with the country's credit rating in 2001/2002 on a par with some developing nations.

Excessive dollar liquidity also had an unintended effect on the U.S.A. Dollar surplus countries (Japan and now China) reinvested their dollar holdings into U.S. assets. Thus a boomerang bubble effect was caused by a massive reflux of dollars back into the U.S., driving up the price of equities, bonds, property and other miscellaneous securities. There was thus an extraordinary Japanese-American symbiosis whereby the Japanese central bank was underwriting U.S. debt in order that the American consumer could purchase their exports (the same process is now happening with China). As Brenner (2002) put it: 'One witnessed the extraordinary spectacle of Japanese financiers providing the credit to the US government to finance its budget deficits in order to subsidize the continuing growth of Japanese exports to the US.' Seeing this, more short-term speculative capital from overseas started to pile in, investment started to boom, the Dow Jones started its remorseless climb, the internet mania took off; this boom – a the New Economic Paradigm – was going to the moon: the roaring 1990s had arrived.

For more sober and seasoned observers, however, this all looked a little worrying. By 1996 even the boss of the Federal Reserve Board, Alan Greenspan, warned of 'irrational exuberance' as the Dow climbed to new highs – bear in mind that this was when the D.J.I.A. stood at around 6000, it was to reach 11500 before the bubble finally burst. But at home and abroad the 1990s roared on. But amidst the euphoria the storm clouds were beginning to gather on the horizon.

After the Japanese bubble had popped there were financial blowouts across the periphery and semi-periphery, involving economies from Brazil to Russia, from Mexico to Malaysia. Excessive liquidity, caused by the injection of huge quantities of U.S. dollars (some two-thirds of central bank foreign currency reserves are comprised of dollars and other U.S. debt instruments) was giving rise to asset price inflation (bubbles) and subsequent busts followed by credit crunches banking crises and slumps. The East Asian financial crisis in 1998 was a good example of this. The liquidity inflow was two-fold: first through trade surpluses, and secondly through speculative short-term credits (hot-money) from outside sources. There followed the usual boom-to-bust cycle.

'According to the figures from the Institute of International Finance, the five East Asian countries hardest hit by the crisis (South Korea, Indonesia, Malaysia, the Philippines and Thailand) experienced in a single year a turnabout of US$105 billion, reaching more than 10% of the GDP of these combined economies; the shift was from an inflow of capital of +US$93 billion in 1996 to an estimated outflow of US$12 billion in 1997. Most of this dramatic swing resulted from commercial bank lending … whilst foreign direct investment remained constant.' (Grieve Smith, J. and Michie, J., *Global Instability*,1999)

Whilst the problem was confined to the periphery and semi-periphery, however, no-body worried too much. The International Monetary Fund (I.M.F.) was sent in to impose its slash and burn, Structural Adjustment Programmes (S.A.P.), together with bail-out loans - which incidentally went straight back into the coffers of those western lending agencies and banks which loaned out the money in the first place. The remit of the I.M.F. was to make sure that western finance was protected and financiers got their money back. However the problem of the dollar glut was beginning to take centre stage.

First World Debt Crisis: Double or Quits.

Given the volume of investment capital moving into the United States during the 1990s, there was considerable G.D.P. growth. However the boom was gradually transmuting into a bubble as the unrelenting rise in asset prices became detached from any realistic valuations. This was particularly true in the case of equities. On Wall Street the profit-to-earnings ratio soared, seemingly beyond the earth's gravitational pull. From a historical norm of 15:1 this ratio had by January 2000 reached the surreal and quite unsustainable level of 44:1. The closest historical parallel to this was just prior to the great crash of 1929 when the ratio stood at 33:1. The glut of investment capital was to result in a generalised over-investment and consequently over-capacity both in the U.S. and abroad - particularly acute in the steel, semi-conductor, automobile and telecommunications equipment industries - which when it arrived tended to have a downward pressure on profit margins and investment.

The bursting of the internet bubble was in a sense inevitable, and as is usual with bubbles was preceded by the most febrile period of runaway growth; G.D.P. was growing by five point two per cent, labour productivity by four point one per cent and non-residential investment by fourteen per cent - heady stuff. However, in the spring of 2000 E-Commerce firms saw their share values collapse and the broader markets began to drop alarmingly. By late winter 2001 the N.A.S.D.A.Q had declined by sixty per cent from its 2000 peak, and pulled down the D.J.I.A. with it. The bubble had popped, $7 trillion had been wiped off the value of shares, and the equity bear market had begun.

However, there was not any corresponding 1930s style slump following in the wake of this financial debacle. This was because the mass of surplus capital exiting the world stock markets was now entering new areas such as bonds and – more importantly – property, creating a new property/consumer credit bubble.

In a grotesque game of double or quits the internet boom and collapse was being supplanted by the property boom on both sides of the Atlantic.

Prognosis

Undoubtedly the engine of world economic growth during the last twenty years has been easy credit (debt) extended to American consumers and businesses. We can call this the Greenspan legacy. In 1980 the ratio of debt to G.D.P. was one hundred and sixty-nine per cent. By 2002 it was two hundred and ninety-two per cent. This consumer spending and brisk business investment powered the growth of the U.S. economy, and through its current account deficits, the U.S. has acted as the locomotive for the world economy - the importer of last resort. It worked like this: the Americans spent $1.06 on imports against $1.00 earned on exports. The principal recipients of this deal have been the East Asian economies and Germany. American consumers do not save; instead they borrow, as does the U.S. government. The $64,000 question is can this Micawberish policy last indefinitely? We will divide the world regionally.

East Asia

Japan seems to have recovered from the (fifteen years) of domestic depression occasioned by the bursting of the great bubble of 1989. What kept the Japanese economy afloat during the lean years was its continuing export success and massive government expenditures. Moreover during the long domestic downturn bad loans were written off, inefficient companies went out of business and the whole bubble distortions and mentality were purged from the system. Japan is now enjoying positive growth rates once more with consumers beginning to spend more freely. These growth rates may not be anything to write home about, but they are soundly based and, given the zero or even negative growth rates of the 1990s, represent a real recovery for the domestic economy.

China continues to grow at a very rapid rate – some nine per cent G.D.P. growth per annum. Its current accumulated dollar surpluses with the U.S. are in the order of $700 billion. This is not an accident: it is the result of the Chinese ministry of trade and finance deciding on a Yuan/Dollar exchange rate resulting in such an outcome. From these surpluses China is able to compete for primary products – e.g. oil – on world markets and also finance its own modernisation. It can also buy up American assets – financial and industrial – if it wishes to do so, although it will (and has) faced some opposition in this respect. The attempt to buy up Unacol, an American energy company was stymied by American opposition. This is symptomatic of tensions bound to build up with the U.S. at some later date – if that is not the case already.

Undoubtedly East Asia is becoming the locus of world capitalist production and liquidity. This is being accompanied by the gradual decline of the North Atlantic powers. But there are problems facing the East Asian economies, namely the massive accumulation of U.S. dollars and dollar-denominated assets. These assets are a very dubious investment since, given their global oversupply they are declining in value. Since the East Asians are reliant on the U.S. export market for their growth and foreign exchange earnings, they have been at pains to support the dollar by the purchase of dollars and U.S. Treasuries. This in effect keeps the value of the Yen and Yuan from appreciating against the dollar and enables the East Asian economies to continue to export and earn further dollar surpluses. However, this means that both the central banks of China and Japan are piling up a mountain of dollars and U.S. Treasury bills which will in the long run collapse anyway. Look at it this way. If the foreign exchange dealers know that someone is willing to buy an overvalued currency they will continue to sell ad infinitum. It is like selling five pound notes for £10. This is what happened when the pound and lira were forced out of the Exchange Rate Mechanism. Selling a currency over its value – i.e. giving money away – will result in a financial tsunami of selling which will overwhelm that currency and lead to its eventual collapse.

The problem for the East Asian economies is that if they sell their surplus dollars now to cut their losses they will in all probability precipitate the very collapse they are at pains to avoid. However, if they do nothing then they will face an even bigger loss at a later date. Additionally, China's continued manipulation of its exchange rate which gives rise to the amassing of U.S. dollars has led to a growth in domestic money supply; necessary in order to buy and convert (some of those) dollars into Yuan. This increased money supply growth will then start to seep into the domestic economy and set off internal inflationary pressures. As has already been noted this is precisely what happened in Japan when property and equity markets rose uncontrollably in the 1980s.

The same tendencies can now be observed in China. If China is to avoid Japan's mistakes it is imperative that it lowers its exposure to dollars; what is beginning to and will continue to happen is a gradual diversification by the East Asian central banks out of the dollar into a basket of currencies and commodities, including gold. China is in the process of abandoning its dollar peg and the Yuan is now being pegged against a basket of currencies including the Euro. Moreover, according to Xinhua News Agency leading Chinese economists, including Teng Tai of China Galaxy Securities company argue that China should increase its gold reserve from 600 tons to about 2,500 tons in the short term and to 3,000 tons in the longer term to reduce the country's reliance on the dollar. At one stage the Euro would have been the obvious alternative to but for political reasons this no longer seems a viable option. China also has to end its reliance on its export-led development strategy with particular reference to its U.S. exports. This will involve the cultivation of an indigenous domestic market and an increasingly regional rather then global focus; although this need not preclude the development of bi-lateral trade agreements and diplomatic connections with overseas countries and regions. In a world hungry for energy supplies China is perforce developing such connexions in countries as far apart as Bolivia (Monroe doctrine or not) and Nigeria.

Japanese intentions are more difficult to gauge. In a purely economistic sense we would expect their future policies not to differ too much from China's. Essentially they face the same dilemma as the Chinese vis-à-vis their American export market and their dollar holdings. Moreover Japan, more than any other East Asian economy, owes a large part of its recent recovery to Chinese growth and Japan's trade surpluses with China. A Japanese regional focus and a cultivation of domestic demand would appear to be the logical policy outcome. However, there are deep-rooted political and national hostilities between the big two East Asian powers. Additionally, Japan is being assiduously courted by the Americans in the time-honoured diplomatic game of divide and rule. Once upon a time the Americans set up Japan as a client state to contain the spread of Chinese communism. Now it appears that Japan is again being set up as a buffer, only this time as a bulwark against Chinese capitalism. The ironies of history! Ultimately, Japan will act in what it considers to be its own best interests; whether this means siding with America rather than China remains to be seen.

The Anglo-Saxon Economies

Looked at in the light of the evidence it really does beggar belief that all the self-congratulatory stuff about these economies blithely ignores that fact that the whole thing was based upon consumers and investors leveraged up to the hilt and equity and property price bubbles – in that order. British consumer spending was roaring along on the easy credit (debt) that led to the property price bubble. By 2005 consumer debt in Britain had reached the equivalent of one hundred and twenty-five per cent of each household's disposable income, or £1.1 trillion. Another worrying statistic turns on the amount borrowed on credit cards. It has risen from £30 million (at today's prices) to £55 billion. The stoking up of house prices stimulated demand and encouraged consumers to borrow to the hilt. This feel-good factor among home-owners which was occasioned by seeing their property grow by twenty per cent per annum (in nominal terms) enabled them to use their homes as A.T.Ms: this Mortgage Equity Withdrawal gave an added momentum to consumer spending. Now, together with private consumer indebtedness, there are increasing government deficits caused by tax shortfalls brought about by the slowdown of the growth rate, and more, longer term problems in the shape of the endowment mortgage fiasco and the looming pensions crisis with companies queuing up to end the final salary schemes. These represent two ticking time-bombs for futures administrations

The U.K. property bubble was absolutely central to the growth between 1997 and 2004. When the Monetary Policy Committee started to raise interest rates to cool down the boom the result was a collapse in consumer demand and a slowdown in growth to an estimated 1.5-2 per cent for the coming year. House prices have since stabilised but are still looking overvalued and are likely to fall further in the longer run.

It is difficult to see how the falling away of growth creating expenditures in the U.K. economy can be boosted by increased aggregate monetary demand. Consumer demand which has kept the economic pot boiling in the UK for the last decade has run into the brick wall of rising interest rates, unsustainable levels of debt and asset price inflation. Consumer spending based upon house-price inflation, has been pushed to its limits and cannot be pushed any further without a very real risk of accelerating inflation, intensifying balance of payments problems and a run on the pound. Stagflation is back on the agenda, and it is difficult to see how growth rates can be sustained in this situation. I should add that Messers Balls and Brown believe it is possible to have permanent growth ('an end to boom and bust') although the Governor of the Bank of England, Mervyn King, takes a different view.

If, by lowering short-term interest rates, the Bank of England can entice U.K. consumers to go even further into debt, then this may be enough to keep demand and consumption going in the next couple of years. But we must be getting very close to the point, if in fact we have not reached it already, when the credit lines and negative savings have reached their limit. The whole cycle now seems to be going into reverse and within a few years (maybe less) the great borrow-and-spend fools' paradise will be no more as the economy continues into its present downturn. This phase of the cycle involves corporate and personal bankruptcies, rising unemployment, home repossessions, negative equity, rising interest rates, government deficits, runs on the pound, deflation/inflation and so forth. Nothing new in this; it is a historically recurring process in the history of capitalism.

On the other side of the pond the U.S. economy has been hostage to three unsustainable trends:

1. The property bubble.
2. The current account deficit.
3. The Federal government budget deficit.

To these we may now add a fourth: the imperial adventure in Iraq, currently estimated to have cost the U.S. up to $2 trillion. These trends have been keeping the U.S. economy – and the world economy – relatively buoyant during the post-internet, stock-market crashes. In addition to the house-price-consumer-credit bubble, there is the current account deficit running at between US$700-800 billion per year – October 2005 was a record month, the bill coming in at $66 billion - this trend is ultimately unsustainable since, according to Peter Schiff, C.E.O. and Chief Global Strategist at Euro Pacific Capital, Inc, on a per capita basis that equates to about $2,300 per person. That is on top of the approximate $40,000 the typical American family already owes the rest of the world. Were the trade deficit to continue at its present level for another ten years the typical family of four would owe approximately $150,000 to the rest of the world.

With regard to government debt the figures are even more mind-boggling. In his analysis John Williams puts forward what can only be described as an apocalyptic view of the level of US government debt. 'For nearly four decades, officially sanctioned accounting gimmicks have masked federal deficit reality. Surpluses in trust accounts, such as Social Security, have been used to obscure the true shortfall in government spending. With less than one tenth of the actual deficit being reported each year, a cumulative negative net worth for the U.S. government has built up in stealth to a level that now tops $45 trillion, with total obligations of $47.3 trillion (more than four times annual G.D.P.) The problem has moved beyond crisis to an uncontrollable disaster that threatens the existence of the U.S. dollar and global financial and economic system. Indeed, the unfolding fiscal nightmare likely will entail a U.S. hyperinflation and a resulting collapse in the value of the world's primary reserve currency, the dollar. With surviving politicians looking to restore public faith in the global currency system, a new system probably will be based on gold, the only monetary asset that has held public confidence for millennia.' (Shadow Government Statistics)

What is notable about these comments is that they come from the heart of the Anglo-American financial and economic establishment. These people are not (funnily enough) socialists or revolutionaries but paid up members of the financial and business elite. That they take a less sanguine and more reasoned view than the type of Pollyanna drivel which is pumped out on a daily basis by mainstream ideologues like Kalestky in *The Times* and Wolf in the *Financial Times* is quite simply because they have to put their money where there mouths are on a daily basis.

The American government will try to keep the bubble going, not least because there are powerful financial lobbies on Wall Street who stand to gain from bubbles, and also since they have now gone past the point where it would be politically feasible for the government to induce a correction. But of course the 'strategy' will ultimately fail for both internal and external reasons. And, as already stated, this judgement is not some lunatic fringe Marxist hysteria; George Soros, for example, has pencilled in 2007 as the year of mayhem. The great American bubble economy can only be kept going if foreign investors believe it to be sustainable. If these investors believe that the dollar must fall against other currencies in order to correct its current account deficit then the dollar will fall. We have already noted that East Asian central banks (beginning with China) are diversifying their portfolios into other currencies – in other words, quietly dumping the dollar. So it really is a question not of 'if' the dollar falls, but when, and by how much it will fall; or whether it will collapse utterly.

Consider the quite plausible scenario: East Asian banks stop buying U.S. Treasury bills and/or other long-dated bonds; U.S. interest rates on these debt instruments will rise dramatically for the reasons given earlier. This means the U.S. house price bubble (that has been playing the same role in terms of driving American growth as has the U.K. property bubble) will pop as the mortgage repayments on already overstretched homeowners rise. Consumer demand would therefore collapse, and the American economy would enter a slump (but not a recession). Along with this the dollar and equity markets would also collapse, and given the role that America's current account deficit has played as consumer of demand for world output, its collapse would be exported to the rest of the globe. This will be the outcome, or should I say nemesis, of Greenspanomics.

The E.U.

For the last ten years at least the principal economic powers in continental Europe – Germany, France and Italy – have been mired in slow growth and high unemployment. This has resulted from the ultra-orthodox monetary and fiscal policies imposed by the European Central Bank (E.C.B.) effectively putting a stranglehold on economic dynamism in the region. This policy was due in large part to

Germany's almost neurotic preoccupation with inflation – no doubt a legacy from the 1923 hyperinflation – and the E.C.B. was to become, in policy terms at least, a facsimile of the old Bundesbank. Although Germany is still a world-beating export performer, it is, like Europe's other underperformers, stuck with the problem of weak domestic demand – a function of an ageing population and a greater propensity to save than the Anglo-Saxon spendthrifts – and the corollary of high unemployment. It should be added at this point that the intention of the new grand coalition government to increase taxes during a period of mass unemployment strikes most economic commentators as ludicrous – a policy which has a striking similarity to the Geoffrey Howe budgets of the early 1980s.

Certainly Europe with many world class companies, high productivity rates – particularly in Western Europe – the size of its internal market (some 320 million people), the size of its G.D.P., and its own regional currency (the Euro) seems to be punching well below its weight in both economic and political terms.

Europe's problems seem to largely stem from a lack of direction and a lack of political vision. From the outset there have been two models of European integration: these may be termed the Gaullist and the Atlanticist. Needless to say the Gaullist vision has waned whilst the Atlanticist vision has waxed. This drift toward an increasingly neo-liberal Europe has been given additional momentum by the inclusion of the former C.O.M.E.C.O.N. states (Hungary, Poland, Czech Republic and so forth). These states are unashamedly Atlanticist in their outlook, cosying up to America at every opportunity. But in a sense the core countries of the E.U. have only themselves to blame for this state of affairs. This is because the inclusion of these new member states into the Union was always a sham. There was never any intention of them being given full membership. Instead Eastern Europe was to be a low-wage hinterland; a peripheral region providing outlets for Western Europe's industry and financial markets, in addition to outsourcing opportunities where lower-end production could be re-located (German companies have been particularly adroit at exploiting this latter opportunity). Eastern Europe was to become Western Europe's Mexico. Euro widening, therefore, should be seen as part of the neo-liberal strategy to both enlarge the area of the customs union and smash the original Delors vision of a social-welfare Europe. Any further additions to the E.U. – and here I am thinking primarily of Turkey – would further consolidate the neo-liberal project.

This is not to say that opposition to this tendency does not exist. To say Europe is totally subordinate to U.S. geo-political strategy is clearly not the case. This was most plainly instanced in the opposition of France and Germany to the Iraq war. But in general social and economic terms the Delors vision of a social-democratic federal Europe seems to be dying a slow death.

Thus Europe flounders on. In policy terms there is both too much integration and not enough: one currency and one interest rate (too much integration); no tax harmonisation or European fiscal policy or exchange rate policy (too little integration). Until there is a consensus about what Europe is for and where it is going and the commensurate institutional structures to facilitate this, the whole Euro project will continue to miscarry – along with the European economy.

Conclusions

One tends to think of economic crises as being one-day cataclysmic events followed by a helter-skleter crash to the bottom. This is not necessarily the case. A crisis can be protracted, taking many years to mature and play itself out; there can also be minor upturns in a situation of generalised downturn. But the general tendency will be one of financial volatility, stagnation, increasing unemployment, inflation or deflation, trade and currency wars, over-capacity, and political and social instability. The U.S., as importer of last resort, has so far staved off global recession; how long this can last is a moot point. The excesses of the roaring 1980s and 1990s will need to be paid for in the form of a massive correction some at time in the future. All this house of cards needs is what, in economists' parlance, is called an exogenous shock. That is to say an unexpected event not necessarily connected with the trade cycle which would be enough to bring the house down, its foundations being rotten. This could be a large bank failure, a surge in commodity prices, or another debacle on the global derivatives market similar to that which happened to the Hedge Fund, Long Term Capital Management. The U.S. monetary authorities – particularly in the form of the departed Alan Greenspan – bear a heavy responsibility for this.

The scene is thus set. All the factors are in place to produce the perfect market correction. Zero savings rate for American consumers, which means there are no savings to dip into during periods of cashflow interruptions or unused credit lines available to them to meet additional needs. No untapped equity built into their homes since they have reached the limits of mortgage equity withdrawal; an economy barely afloat in an endless sea of debt which would quickly drown under the weight of higher interest rates; no base of well-paid employment to act as a life preserver to ride out the storm. No further reliance on foreign borrowing since that has been exhausted anyway. Nor is increasing government borrowing a possibility given the government's present gargantuan liabilities.

In Go(l)d we trust

As an indicator of the present condition of the global economy a look at the markets for precious metals is very instructive. Since the bottom of the internet bust c.2001 the price of gold has climbed inexorably. Platinum has risen from $400 an ounce in October 2001 to its present twenty-five year high. These are not just temporary price spikes; something more fundamental is happening. People – particularly in the speculative and financial community – are losing their trust in fiat (paper or credit) money. In the trade this is called 'hedging'. Investors are lowering their exposure to paper currencies in their portfolios and increasing their holdings of precious metals. Given the world is submerged in a sea of fiat money its value becomes increasingly problematic. The value of precious metals is not. They have been recognised as a store of value for over two thousand years and at times of crisis there is always a movement of capital into these particular commodities. People may not trust paper money or central bankers, but they trust gold. On the back of the American currency is the motto: In God We Trust. Please note the above amendment.

What is happening in the bullion markets represents the first rumblings of the seismic indicator before the earthquake.

The present protracted crisis is truly global and interlocking since no country or region will be unaffected by the reconfiguration which has to take place in the American economy. This is particularly the case with those countries that have strong export markets within the U.S. The Chinese economy for one will be virtually stopped in its tracks by an internal U.S. contraction. Also affected will be Japan and the other East Asian economies as well as Germany, albeit to a lesser extent.

In summation it seems that we are approaching an historical turning point; the counter-revolutionary momentum built up during the 1980s and 1990s seems to be breaking on the shoals of economic reality. We have been living on borrowed time and borrowed money; the bills are now rolling in. The party, if not actually over, seems to be approaching endgame. It would appear that all the variants of late capitalism: the Rhineland, East Asian and now Anglo-American models, were all systemically flawed. The East Asian economies are excessively export dependent and vulnerable to a fall-off of demand for their goods in their principal export market, the U.S.; the E.U. area seems destined to continue on the path of low growth and high unemployment given the internecine spats, cringing before the U.S., and Bourbon-like posture of the principal actors. And the Anglo-American economies are bloated property/credit bubbles waiting to burst: which they will. The longevity and severity of this downturn will be in proportion to the excesses of the bubble period. It is like Newton's Third Law of Physics: 'for every action there is an equal and opposite reaction.' After the great meltdown the world that emerges will be fundamentally reconfigured: the pendulum may well have overshot before it moves back to its equilibrium position. American debts will be written down by hyperinflation of the dollar, but the dollar will no longer be the global reserve currency – in fact it will be something of a pariah currency. The global reserve currency may turn out to be the Euro after all, or there will be the re-emergence of a de facto gold standard. American global dominance will be no more. As the French say: "Tout passé, tout casse. Everything goes away. Everything breaks down. Nothing is born that does not die. Nothing begins that does not end. There is no morning without an evening, and no silver lining without a cloud. Empires come, empires go."

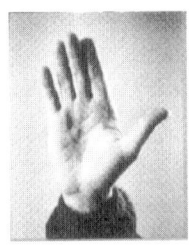 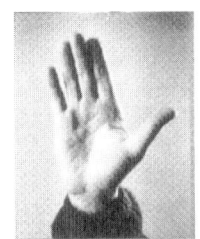 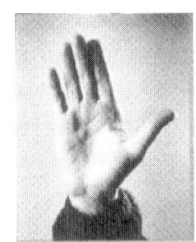

Section 2: History

Few would argue that Tony Blair will leave office safe in the knowledge that he followed his convictions. But his decade-or-so-long tenure at the helm of Labour is but a mere blink of the eye in a long and proud libertarian socialist tradition.

In the following essay, Duncan Bowie sets out the history of this tradition, as without it we cannot truly seek to avoid falling into the same pitfalls or share the same successes.

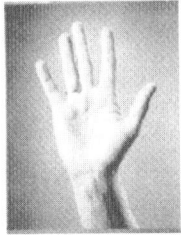 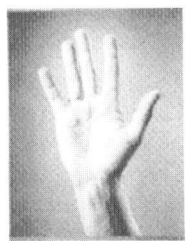 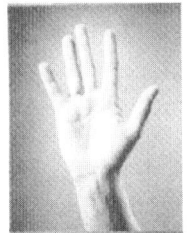

Far from a one-trick ideology:

A brief history of the libertarian socialist tradition

Duncan Bowie

Preface

Chartist is not only part of the democratic socialist tradition: it is part of a libertarian tradition. In contrast with the anarchist tradition, we do see a role for the state and for forms of representative government, but we also recognize that the power of the state should be limited and the liberties of individuals protected so far as they do not conflict with the liberties of others. In advocating collective rather than individualist approaches to society, we advocate grass roots approaches to collectivism rather than imposed uniformity and leveling. In recognizing the role of the state in enabling the achievement of both equality of opportunity and greater equality of both wealth and income, we recognize that representative democracy has to operate at a number of levels from the local to the international. We therefore support the principle of subsidiarity – that political and economic decisions are made at the most localized level which is effective – this recognizes that decisions about the distribution of political power between world regions can only be made at the international level – but that even at this level, decision making can and must operate on the basis of representative democracy.

Some readers may question whether socialist history is of relevance to contemporary political debates. With a government neo-liberal in its economic policy, authoritarian and centralist in its domestic policy and neocolonialist in its approach to other countries and the international community, it is important to reassert the socialist tradition. Current political life has no memory. For a new generation, socialism like communism is consigned to the history books as something dead and buried and of no contemporary significance. A reassertion of socialist principles is necessary to demonstrate the extent to which Blair and New Labour are antipathetic to socialist principles. It is however also necessary to demonstrate that the crude characterizations of socialism as state control and state-imposed leveling are not representative of the diversity within the socialist tradition.

Part 1. From utopian socialism to the First International

It is arguable that the libertarian socialist tradition can be dated from the radical reformation of the levelers and diggers in England or from the Hussites and Anabaptists in sixteenth-century Holland, Germany and Bohemia. These movements combined radical interpretations of the gospel with a revolt against both ecclesiastical and monarchical governance. However if modern socialism is seen to originate from the works of Robert Owen in England and Saint Simon in France, then we need to start with the alternatives to their statist and centralist versions of socialism which were advocated by some of their contemporaries. Both Saint Simon and Owen were systematisers who developed their concepts of a socialist organization of society into a set of rules and physical plans, which were to be imposed on communities. Both reformers saw themselves as enlightened benefactors bringing wisdom to the unenlightened working class. Both appealed to monarchs and to the aristocracy for support for their systems as much aimed at bringing the threatening lower orders under some form of societal control as at bringing benefits to the lower orders themselves.

Not all of Owen's and Saint Simon's followers were content with being instruments of a dictator, however benevolent that dictator may be. Owen provided support for both local co-operative stores and for early trade union organization. Many of the mechanics and artisans involved in these projects developed their own political understanding based on daily engagement in production and distribution. William Lovett and Francis Place, both early Chartists, were deeply involved in Owenite organizations. In the columns of Owenite journals such as the *New Moral World and the Crisis*, the latter being the journal of Owen's Grand National Consolidated Trade Union, can be found reports of local educational and trade union activity operating autonomously of any central direction. Owenite social missionaries such as Charles Southwell presented their own interpretations of Owen's message, focusing on the political and economic arguments for socialism. Local co-operatives and unions would publish their own journals – such as *The Pioneer* in Birmingham, while in Manchester, Rowland Detroisier argued for 'moral and political instruction among the working classes' through mechanics institutes, as the basis of political advancement.

In France, Saint Simon was only one of a number of utopian thinkers. Charles Fourier developed his more libertarian if somewhat eccentric approach to social organization, which centred on adapting the role of individuals in work and society to their individual passionate characteristics, while Etienne Cabet developed his own concept of societal organisation through his Icarian phalansteries – it was Cabet who, a decade before Marx's communist manifesto, introduced the notion of communist organization. In France there was also a strong tradition of catholic co-operatives and associationism, given intellectual leadership by the socialist Pierre Leroux, and the former Simonian and Carbonari, Philippe Buchez.

In England, Chartism in the later 1830s and 1840s was a very different kind of movement from Owenism. While the original charter of 1838 was a joint product of The London Working Mens Association and a group of sympathetic radical Members of Parliament, the movement was primarily an agitation for independent working class political representation and owed little to any middle class sponsorship – in fact much of Chartism was as antagonistic to the middle class as it was to the monarchy and the aristocracy. The radical Chartists however saw economic power as important as political power and realized that they needed to take independent action as well as just providing a critique of the status quo – thus the ill-fated Chartist Land Company set up by Fergus O'Connor, which aimed to give workers control of land to enable them to reap the rewards of their own efforts as farmers. Moderate Chartists, including Lovett and Holyoake who had been heavily influenced by Owen, in contrast turned to education and temperance campaigns as the basis for working class advancement. Many Chartist leaders did however become political leaders, either in local politics or in national trade union or Liberal politics – some becoming active in the First International.

The role of the state in assisting the development of socialism moved quickly from being an issue of theoretical debate to an issue of practical politics, which brought the socialist Louis Blanc, author of the seminal tract on the *Right to Work*, into the position of Minister of Labour in the French republican government of 1848. In this role he established a Labour Commission at the Palais de Luxembourg which adopted the principle of employment for all based on a minimum wage. The subsequent months provided a vigorous debate between the advocates of state organization of labour, primarily to ensure the workers were preoccupied and less likely to riot, and advocates of worker control of production – Blanc despite his position supporting the latter, while rivals in Government established national workshops based on the former principle.

Much has been written on the contest in the First International between Marx and anarchists led first by Proudhon and then by Bakunin. The fascination in reading the minutes of the early meetings of the London-based General Council, is the range of arguments and issues covered, with Marx's position only one of many and not always the dominant one. In this context it should be noted that not only Proudhon in France had adopted an anti-statist form of socialism, with his focus on mutuality of wealth and credit, but both Herzen in Russia and Colins, Kats and de Kayser in Belgium were advocating collective ownership of land and capital and the establishment of systems of self-governing communes with central government playing a purely administrative role. Colins also argued for the abolition of inheritance, state control of education and following Blanc, a public works programme to minimize unemployment. It is consequently not surprising that debates over inheritance and land ownership featured prominently on the agenda of the First International. Marx did not necessarily win the economic arguments, even though he was at that time drafting the first sections of his work on Capital. Trade unionists were not convinced that either mechanism or higher wages were preconditions for a social system of production. The first conference of the International took the Proudhonist line in support of credit societies despite Marx's opposition. At one stage, the French trade union delegates proposed that membership the International be limited to manual workers, and that intellectuals such as Marx should be excluded. The International supported the abolition of inheritance despite Marx's comment that this was the worst way to start a revolution. Marx and Eccarius advocated reduced hours of labour, but were opposed by British trade unionists concerned that this would just reduce wages. At the Geneva Congress of 1866, the Council actually agreed to try to prohibit female manual labour despite Marx arguing that women and children had an equal duty to work. The Proudhonists also successfully argued that a moral basis for society was as important as the economic basis advocated by Marx. The 1868 congress, missed by Marx, was won over by the arguments of the Belgian Cesar de Paepe, to support a general strike against war – an idea Marx considered to be stupid – but also to support the nationalization of land, mines and railways. De Paepe's view of collective ownership was that while land and industry would be owned by the state, it would be let to companies of working men. At the Basle congress of 1869, De Paepe's colleague Hins went as far as to argue that the trade unions should themselves take over the organization of society and that there was no need for the state – an early advocacy of syndicalism.

Bakunin's intervention in the International has been the subject of many studies. What is often forgotten is the extent to which Bakunin's anti-authoritarianism and his opposition to state control chimed with the views of many continental socialists but also those British trade unionists such as John Weston and John Hales who had remained active in the International. Some of the more established trade unionists such as Howell and Cremer distanced themselves from Marx's position, and later from the International itself as Marx supported the violence of the Paris commune. Had it not been for the commune, it is likely that the International would have supported the Belgian-led collectivist agenda – the Mainz congress was due to debate for the first time a comprehensive political programme – the collectivization of land, abolition of public debts, establishment of national banks, co-operative production, the abolition of standing armies and the 'connection between the political action and the working class': all policies Marx either opposed or saw as irrelevant. The outbreak of the Franco-German war not just led to the cancellation of the congress but in effect blocked the political and theoretical development of the International.

The defeat of the commune not only destroyed the French working class movement but it also weakened the International. Marx struggled against Bakunin to maintain control over an organisation now little more than a rump of London-based exiles. When De Paepe's compromise of condemning secret societies while keeping some of the anarchists and anti-statists within the organization was carried as was a proposal to support political action initiated by French Blanquist Eduard Vaillant at the London conference of 1871, the General Council, still controlled by Marx and Eccarius, failed to follow up the resolution, and the British internationalists, led by Hales and influenced at least in part by Proudhon's 1863 on the Principle of Federation, set up their own federal council. This held its own congress and adopted its own political programme – adult suffrage, land nationalization, free education, disestablishment of the church, establishment of a national bank and abolition of the aristocracy and the magistracy – a programme that provoked an attack by Marx. Marx then tried to impose central control over the national councils – opposed by the English federalists and the Belgians as well as by Bakunin and his supporters. In desperation, he decided the only way to save the International from the federalists and anarchists was to transfer the International's headquarters to New York, which in effect meant winding up the organization. However despite Marx's action, de Paepe and the Belgians made attempts to keep the continental socialists, collectivists, federalists and anarchists together. An 1877 conference at Ghent was attended by Liebknecht as well as British federalists John Hales and Maltman Barry, Paul Brousse from France and Kropotkin. After Ghent the anarchists, led by Guillaume in Switzerland, held a series of international conferences, some attended by Belgian collectivists. One product of this continuing collaboration was a debate in 1874 between De Paepe and the Swiss Schwitzguebel of the Jura Federation, on the collective organisation of public services and the role of the state. De Paepe argued that services should be organized by individual communes, except for services common to more than one commune such as railways and the postal service, which should be organized by a federation of communes. These could operate at a regional or national level – and in effect were forms of state: 'Instead of the Jacobin notion of the all-powerful state, we offer the idea of the liberated commune, itself appointing all its administrators, with no exceptions: shifting for itself in respect of laws, justice and police. The liberal conception of the gendarme state we counter with the notion of the state disarmed, but charged with educating the young and centralizing the great undertakings. The commune becomes essentially the organ of political functions or what are described as such: law, justice, security, the guaranteeing of contracts, the protection of the incapable, civic society, but at the same time it is the organ of all public services. The State in essence becomes the organ of scientific unity and of the great joint undertakings necessary to society.'

Schwitzguebel's response was positive: 'Two principles, of immeasurable historical import, have emerged from the debates and internal squabbling which caused upset within our Association: the principle of collective ownership, as the economic bass of the new organization of society, and the principle of autonomy and federation, as the basis of upon which human individuals and collectivities are banded together.'

In the battle between Marxian centralism and Bakunist anarchism which split the First International, and was to divide the Second International as well, the basic principles of libertarian socialism stand out as a rational basis for political and economic action.

Part 2: Challenges to statist socialism in the period of the Second International

Just as Marx had been challenged by a range of alternative interpretations of socialism within the First International, so Engels and the defenders of Marxist orthodoxy in the early years of the Second International faced a range of challenges. Historians tend to have focused on the revisionism of Bernstein and Volmar and the disputes with the anarchists. This however hides a wider range of tendencies both within and beyond the European socialist movement. Nevertheless it should be recognized that even the defenders of orthodoxy, Kautsky and Bebel, rejected the concepts of an imposed revolutionary dictatorship, the approach later adopted by Lenin that perhaps owed more to Weitling and Blanqui than it did to Marx. In 1891, Kautsky argued that freedom of association, freedom of assembly and a free press, were essential to the achievement of socialism – 'These freedoms are of prime importance to the working class, they represent the vital conditions of existence without which the [working] class itself cannot develop, These freedoms are light and air for the proletariat and whoever restricts them, rejects them, or tries to divert the workers from the struggle to win and broaden them is among the worst enemies of the proletariat, whatever great love of the proletariat he may feel or feign.' Kautsky placed his Marxism on firm democratic foundations, which explains why later he was to strongly oppose Leninist centralism. Kautsky's colleague Bebel took up the challenge Marx had ducked, of providing an outline of a future socialist society. In his 1879 work on Women and Socialism, he argued that the proletariat would be emancipated in terms of both economic and social relations, with 'labour organized on the basis of complete freedom and democratic equality'. Extending Engel's concept of the 'withering away of the state', Bebel argued that with the end of the state, 'disappear its representatives: ministers, parliaments, regular armies, police and gendarmes, courts, lawyers and public prosecutors, prison wardens, tax inspectors and customs authorities, in a word – the whole political apparatus. Barracks and other military buildings, court and administrative premises, prisons etc will be turned to better use. Tens of thousands of laws, decrees and regulations will be turned to better use.' However Bebel was no more an anarchist than de Paepe, and recognized the need to create an alternative governmental structure, consisting of administrative collegiums and delegations with responsibilities for organizing production and distribution, communication systems, industry and agriculture, art and education. Bebel, the 'orthodox Marxist', appears to adopt a Fourierist utopianism – not only will all matters will be dealt with objectively as no one would have personal interests opposed to society, but with the abolition of conflict of interest, poverty and crime would also be abolished. Not surprisingly, Bebel's vision was to be widely promoted by the English socialists, especially the ethical socialists, in the 1890s and 1900s.

While Bebel was promoting utopian ideals of a socialist paradise, it was socialists coming from the anarchist tradition who were carrying out the most systematic and realistic analysis of the nature of future socialist organization. Moving on from the confused economics and philosophy of the early Proudhon and the crude anti-authoritarianism of Bakunin with its nihilist connotations, anarcho-communists such as Kropotkin and Elisee Reclus developed a strategy for political action which was not limited to the focus on elections and parliamentary institutions of the German social democrats who dominated the International. Bakunin and Reclus, with their colleagues in the Swiss-based Jura Federation, argued that the produce of labour should be collectively owned as well as the instruments of labour, and that distribution should reflect need not just labour. Kropotkin argued that Marxian collectivism, based on the use of compulsion to enforce work, would re-establish a wage structure that replicated the authoritarianism of capitalist society. Kropotkin's voluntarism, set out most fully in his work on 'Mutual Aid', was predicated on the theory that the human race had a propensity to co-operation. This theory derived largely from the fact that Kropotkin and Reclus were both geographers and anthropologists and provided an alternative scientific basis to communism to the economic and philosophical based scientific socialism of Marx. It was the basis of Kropotkin's development of an anarchist morality as well as establishing the principles of anarcho-communist approaches to government, law and authority, political organization and revolutionary change. Kropotkin believed that the state was responsible for conflict. Pointing to the success of voluntary cooperative enterprises, he argued that progress was most effective where there was no state interference: anarchism would 'guarantee economic freedom without reducing the individual to the role of a slave to the state – a further advance in social life does not lie in the direction of a further concentration of power and regulatory functions in the hands of a governing body, but in the direction of decentralization, both territorial and functional.' Kropotkin was vigorously opposed to the Blanquist notion of the revolutionary dictatorship – 'every dictatorship leads, even the best intentioned, to the death of all revolutionary movement'. As a historian of the French revolution of 1789-83, he believed that the role of secret societies was to prepare peoples minds for the revolution, but not to lead the revolution or to govern after the revolution. Revolution 'is not a simple change of governors. It is the taking possession by the people of all social wealth. It is the abolition of all the forces which have so long hampered the development of humanity… It is necessary that the people should have their hands free, that they act according to their own will, and march forward without waiting for orders from anyone… It is this very thing which a dictatorship would prevent.' Kropotkin's 1880 pamphlet on Revolutionary Government is a fascinating anticipation of the arguments over the Bolshevik revolution of October 1917.

The development of socialism in Britain also owed little to Marxist orthodoxies being based essentially on ethical and dissenting religious traditions. In the middle and late nineteenth century English radicalism had been led by dissenting and secularist traditions, from Carlyle, through Linton and Holyoake to Bradlaugh. The new socialist movement was born out of the radical working class clubs in London, with even Hyndman's Democratic Federation mainly comprising survivors of the Chartist, republican and land nationalisation movements, with only Hyndman and Belfort Bax having some familiarity with Marx and the German Hegelians.

William Morris also came to socialism through ethics rather than through economics. For Morris, capitalism was barbarous in that it limited the individual's natural right to dignity and self-expression. It was only through an egalitarian society that self-expression, culture and beauty could blossom. Inequality was a waste of human and material resources. In rejecting 'mechanical power' Morris sought a return to a romantic idealization of a medieval village based society, based on the principle of voluntary co-operation with the minimum of government. In the utopia he expounded in *News from Nowhere*, private property was abolished; equality of material considerations had been achieved. External restraint on the individual, law police and government were removed. The new society depended on man's natural urge towards 'fellowship' and 'association'. Society was to be governed by a collective 'social conscience'. Morris's ideal society was 'the freedom and cultivation of the individual will, which civilization ignores...; the shaking off of the slavish dependence on artificial systems.' There was a strong libertarian trend within Morris's Socialist League, and the League soon became dominated by a semi-anarchist group. One individual however stands out in this group: Joseph Lane, a London radical and socialist, secretary of the Stratford Radical and Dialectical Club in the 1880s and 1890s. Lane had been active in a number of earlier radical campaigns – the Land Tenure Reform Association formed by John Stuart Mill, Charles Dilke's republican campaign to be M.P. for Chelsea, the Manhood Suffrage League and the Rose Street Social Democratic Club in Soho. He then set up the Labour Emancipation League, one of whose activities was a campaign to re-establish the First International. Joining Morris's Socialist League, Lane led the faction that opposed parliamentary participation. As part of this campaign, he wrote *An Anti-Statist Communist Manifesto*: 'The object of socialism is to constitute a society founded on labour and science, on liberty equality and solidarity of all human beings. We are waging a battle of labour against capital... We pursue a warfare of freedom against authority... We champion the cause of producers as arrayed against that of the non-producers... We fight the battle of equality against privilege.'

The revived socialist movement in Britain drew heavily on the arguments of the American Henry George, who in his seminal work *Progress and Poverty*, borrowing from the arguments of the Spenceans a hundred years earlier, argued that individual ownership of natural wealth, primarily land, was morally unjust. Coming from a religious tradition, he believed that as all were equal in the eyes of God then all had an equal right to the use of all natural wealth. Though George never saw himself as a socialist, in many ways he was the most successful advocate of socialism in the late nineteenth century, with commitment to land reform acting as a bridge between radicals and socialists. Ethical arguments also played a part in the development of socialist politics on the continent. Although orthodox Marxism dominated the German socialist movement and the French socialist group led by Guesde, there were a wide range of traditions and Marxism failed to dominate the movement in Spain, Italy or indeed France. While Italian and Spanish left politics were dominated by a conflict between Marxism and anarchism, it is in France that the ethical tradition was strongest. For example, Jean Jaures, radical parliamentarian and then founder of the united French Socialist Party, came to socialism with an ethical and humanist perspective. Philosopher and historian, he saw socialism as the realization of a universal harmony representing the progress of society towards the adoption of ideals. He regarded the advent of socialism as a 'great religious revolution' – a revolution of justice and goodness. He denied that any conflict existed between collectivism and individual freedom – social institutions could only be based on individual values and without individual will social institutions would have no vitality. Socialism could be achieved and socialist institutions could be established when the majority of the population recognized that socialism represented the true human values. He therefore rejected insurrection and insisted that the social revolution could only succeed if preceded by moral changes.

Marxism, anarcho-communism and ethical socialism were not mutually exclusive tendencies. As has been shown already many of the most influential socialist thinkers bridged traditions – both Bebel and Bax incorporated ethical and even utopian arguments. Two communards, Guesde and Brousse, were to move away from anarchism – Guesde to Marxist orthodoxy, Brousse to a reformist socialism. Perhaps the best example of a socialist transcending a number of traditions was Benoit Malon, also a communard and editor of the *Revue Socialiste* – never a factional leader but educator and advisor to a generation of French socialists, and author of the seminal work *Le Socialisme Integral*. Malon had learnt from the experience of the commune and the anarchist agitation of the post-commune years that not only was the revolution not imminent but that a revolution would not automatically achieve a socialist society. He therefore advocated social reforms such as reduced working hours, recognizing that such campaigns would raise the workers consciousness and prepare them for more radical change. He stressed the importance of winning control of municipalities and argued that municipal enterprise could 'lay the basis of communal property and prepare the grand socialist federation of communes.' He advocated a form of decentralized socialism and a non-dogmatic socialist party and therefore opposed the authoritarianism and centralism advocated by Guesde. Malon instead supported the attempt by Paul Brousse to prepare a municipal programme as a libertarian socialist alternative to the Mimimum Programme which had been drafted by Guesde with Engel's assistance. Brousse called for the collective management of public services to meet the needs of the working class and for the capture of municipal control through electoral participation. The manifesto included a detailed list of reforms to be undertaken by the socialist commune, in contrast the Guesdist programme which comprised a series of demands on central government. While Brousse explicitly rejected revolution, he nevertheless insisted on the proletariat being a distinct class and distinct political party. The Possibilist Party which he founded and which Malon supported was not reformist in the sense of seeking to revise Marxist fundamentals – the preamble of the Possibilist programme adopted in 1885 confirmed in orthodox Marxist terms that the emancipation of the workers can only be the work of the workers themselves and that capital was the origin of all slavery – political, moral and material. The economic emancipation of the workers was the end to which the whole political movement was subordinated. It was not however the objective to turn the proletariat into a new privileged class but to realize equality for all. This constituted true freedom. The Possibilist programme therefore combined the economics of Marxism, the moral basis of ethical socialism, the arguments for a decentralized political structure from the anarcho-communists, the collectivism of de Paepe and the traditional republican objectives of equality and liberty.

The views of Malon and Brousse were not dissimilar from those of Emile Vandervelde, leader of the Belgian socialists and secretary of the Socialist International. Building on the Belgian federalist tradition, Vandervelde advocated collectivism and the role of the commune and saw the socialist party as an alliance of trade unions, cooperatives and other working class organizations, rather than as a monolithic centrally-directed body. He wrote a book *Socialism Against the State* which argued that socialism must be constructed politically, economically and culturally by working class organizations and not imposed by the state. By using Marxist terminology, Vandervelde avoided allegations of revisionism – moreover he not only kept the Belgian Socialist Party united but acted as a reconciler between competing tendencies within the International, as well as later becoming a minister in the Belgian coalition government. It was his ability to combine the positive aspects of different traditions, to relate theory to political practice and to recognize the importance of the link between the means by which socialism was achieved and the form which socialist society would take, that makes his contribution so important. Brousse, Malon and Vandervelde all believed that through the communes and within socialist organizations themselves, the future socialist society could be prefigured within the capitalist and bourgeois but democratic state – a position that linked work for a socialist future to specific and actual socialist achievements in the present – possible in a liberal democracy but less tenable in an autocratic state, which goes some way to explain why such an optimistic theoretical position based on a peaceable transition towards socialism was regarded by Lenin, Martov and other Russian Marxists as both utopian and naïve.

Before commenting on the reassertion of the insurrectionist tradition through Lenininism, it is necessary to touch on revisionist tendencies within the Second International and seek to relate them to the libertarian tradition. Revisionism has often been used as a term of abuse by followers of the Marxist tradition who believe in a concept of orthodoxy, deviation from which is heretical. This fails to recognize that given the range of arguments propounded by Marx and Engels, their writings are open to a range of interpretations. The main distinction to be drawn between ethical socialists and revisionists is that the former drew on pre-Marxist traditions while the latter were post-Marxists in that they acknowledged Marx and Engels' contribution while explicitly reinterpreting or modifying it. In this sense it was the Fabian Society in Britain who were the first socialist group to critically but sympathetically examine the economic works of Marx only to find them wanting. The focus of the Fabians' early work was however a commitment to collectivism and it was Sidney Webb who inserted the explicitly socialist commitments into the Labour Party constitution in 1918. While the Webbs in later years were seen as the leading advocates in Britain of statist socialism in the period before the First World War, they were the leading advocates of municipal collectivism, with public services provided by local authorities and other locally accountable bodies, trialling their initiatives in the London County Council. They were, however, not enthusiasts for worker self-management – services were to be provided by experts based on minimum standards set and enforced by the state. While being advocates of municipal collectivism, the early Fabians do not sit easily within a libertarian socialist tradition, and it was the Fabian focus on the leadership role of the intellectual which bears some comparison with the attitude of Lenin to the relationship between vanguard and the masses that in fact provoked the guild socialist reaction of the post war years.

Similarly the revisionism of Bernstein, who developed his ideas in London Fabian circles, was primarily a critique of Marx's assumptions on the development and collapse of capitalism which led him to reject the concept of the dictatorship of the proletariat. While he did criticize centralised bureaucracy and argued for a 'democracy based on elaborately organized self government', his support for an alliance with Liberals and defence of colonialism, two tendencies shared with leading Fabians, also take him outside the libertarian tradition. The modifications made by the socialist group in Russia known as the 'economists' are however more significant if less well known, as their modification of Marxism had the objective of achieving a peaceful transition to socialism in an autocratic state. The 'economist' Kuskova, following the argument of the Bundists (the Russian Jewish Socialist Party) and Arkadi Kramer and Julius Martov in their pamphlet *On Agitation*, argued in her *Credo* (published in 1899) that the theoretical Marxists of the R.S.D.L.P. were in fact isolating themselves from the working class and that socialist progress depended on both the self-education of the working class and their active participation in both workplace organization and political reform movements. The 'economists' were seeking to focus political agitation on the most effective channels. It should also be noted that in a country that was predominantly rural, both the intellectual class and the industrial proletariat were minorities, with the peasants actually being the majority of the population. Both factions within the R.S.D.L.P. failed to take account of the interests and the potential role of the peasantry, whose main political representation was through the Social Revolutionary Party or S.R. It is significant that the S.R. took a much more decentralized approach to the organisation of government, supporting communal social ownership of land rather than centralized state ownership as well as advocating forms of communal self government. The objectives and political practice of the S.R. contrasted with the political opportunism and vanguardism of the Leninists and the dogmatic proletarianism and statism of the Mensheviks.

Lenin was not the first proponent of the catastrophic theory of the advance of socialism – the belief that capitalism society would collapse as it over-reached itself. He followed a succession of socialist thinkers from the German Parvus, the Austrian Hilferding, the Pole Luxemburg and the English radical imperialist Hobson. Lenin's achievement was to combine the theories of capitalist collapse, the role of a vanguard party and the Blanquist notion of insurrection leading to a dictatorship of the proletariat. In practice Leninism was the dictatorship of a faction of the socialist movement over the proletariat, peasantry and bourgeoisie. The only comment that needs to be made in a paper on the libertarian socialist tradition is that Leninist theory and practice was counter to it. In terms of political practice in the revolutionary period, Trotsky, despite coming from the more democratic Menshevik tradition, differed little from Lenin and can also be considered as antipathetic to the libertarian tendency.

This takes us swiftly on to the syndicalism of the decade before the First World War, the last of the major tendencies of the Second International period. As a theory of socialist organization, syndicalism was primarily a product of the specific circumstances in the French socialist movement in the years after the commune. The revival of the labour movement was based not on a fragmented national political movement but on the development of local workplace based trade union organization. Local trade union militants were influenced by the federalist and municipalist traditions of Proudhon and the Broussists, but as industrial organizers they focused on control of production rather than the self-governing commune. Industrial action was prioritized over political action. As developed by the prominent Pelloutier, syndicalist theory was predicated on a socialist society being achieved through a general strike rather than through a political revolution. The education of workers for power was to be undertaken through trade unions not trough political parties. The workers had a capacity for self-government – there was no need for an intellectual vanguard. The industrial unionism of De Leon in the United States shared the syndicalist emphasis on industrial organization but considered that workplace organisation needed to be directed by a political party which adopted a vanguardist approach. While the French syndicalists focused on local organization, De Leon advocated one big union – nationally and internationally. It was contact with the American De Leonite Socialist Labour Party that led to a faction splitting from the British Social Democrat Federation to found a British Socialist Labour Party (S.L.P.), forming the Advocates of Industrial Unionism as a parallel body to the Industrial Workers of the World – the I.W.W. or Wobblies. The British S.L.P. was even more sectarian than its American model and had little influence. Nevertheless syndicalist ideas found a prominent advocate in Tom Mann, former secretary of the Independent Labour Party, who returned from Australia to Britain in 1910 having been converted to industrial unionism by industrial struggles in the antipodes. He established a journal – the *Industrial Syndicalist* – and organized lecture tours and a national conference. Syndicalist arguments were adopted by a number of trade unionists in the pre-war period when industrial action became widespread – advocated by a number who had been students at Oxford's Ruskin College (which for a brief period was run as a student and lecturer syndicate) and then by a group of Ruskin-educated miners leaders in South Wales led by Noah Ablett, who published the pamphlet *The Miners' Next Step*. Syndicalist approaches were adopted by agitators in other countries who also disputed Marx's limited view on the role of industrial organization, including the Italian Antonio Labriola, the Dutchman Domela Niuwenhuis, Henry Holland in New Zealand and Ervin Szabo in Hungary. Szabo was most critical of participation in parliamentary politics which he saw as inevitably creating a new leadership who would exclude the working class movement from power rather than represent its interests. Syndicalism did seek to create through the trade union organisation a structure that challenged the existing state institutions, assisted the development of the class struggle, and prefigured the structure of the anticipated socialist society. As a contribution to socialist theory and practice, the role of syndicalism should not be undervalued. Syndicalism represented not just a call to action but a belief in self-education through struggle.

Part 3: After Leninism

With the rise of Leninism, the establishment of the Third International and the growth of Leninist communist parties across Europe and beyond, libertarian socialist traditions became forgotten and libertarian socialist tendencies became marginalized. In the struggle between the reformist Second International and Leninist Third International, alternative socialist tendencies were weakened and dissipated. Many of the post-Leninist movements tend to be seen as reactions against Leninism rather than positive ideologies in their own right. The main ideological struggle was between the social reformism of the English and German labour movements, supporting the Menshevik exiles, and the new communist movements sponsored by Soviet Russia. One of the few independent socialist parties – the Independent Socialist or U.S.P.D. in Germany – was soon to fraction. The Independent Labour Party in England went through a similar split. French politics also became polarised after the 1920 Tours conference between communist and reformism. Those on the left who did not support the new revolution were often hesitant to be too critical of the new Russia for fear of being seen as traitors allied to the White reaction. Some hesitancy was due to an instinctive sympathy with the Russian leadership fighting against both economic and external forces and a wish to give the Soviet a chance to get through the transitional period.

There were critiques of Leninism from a libertarian perspective. Some came from the anarchist tradition – from Kropotkin, Emma Goldman and Sacha Berkman; others from the orthodox marxist tradition of Kautsky and the Mensheviks. One of the soundest critiques however came from a libertarian socialist perspective from the English philosopher Bertrand Russell. Russell had already published in 1918 *Roads to Freedom* which, in a study of Marxism, anarchism and syndicalism, had shown strong sympathy for the syndicalist position. In 1920, after visiting Russia attached to a British Labour part official tour, he wrote *The Practice and Theory of Bolshevism*. He was critical of the Bolshevik attitude to democracy and its use of violence to impose a dictatorship – not of the proletariat, but of the Bolshevik party over the proletariat. Russell was not himself convinced that an alternative approach would be successful in achieving radical reform. However he concluded: 'equalization of wealth without equalization of power seems to me a rather small and unstable achievement. But equalization of power is not a thing that can be achieved in a day. It requires a considerable level of moral, intellectual and technical education. It requires a long period without extreme crises, in order that habits of tolerance and good nature may become common.'

In his polemic, Russell also argued: 'self-government in industry is an indispensable condition of a good society'. This was the objective of the British guild socialist movement. This rather romantically named group combined the objectives of the pre-war syndicalists with a Christian socialist tradition and an idealized and retrospective view of medieval artisan society. The first book, *The Restoration of the Gild System*, was actually published before the war – by Arthur Penty in 1906, a book that in its preface referred back to Ruskin, Carpenter, Carlyle and Matthew Arnold. The use of the term 'Restoration' is symbolic of the fact that Penty was rejecting modern industrialized society and saw a medieval collectivism as the only salvation for a society 'wallowing in the troughs of commercialism'. Later advocates were more practical if less prosaic. G.D.H. Cole, who during the war had undertaken a study of self-government in industry, in his 1920 work *Social Theory* endorsed the guild socialist perspective as the basis for a new system of social organization: 'I assume that the object of social organization is not merely the material efficiency, but also essentially the fullest self-expression of all the members...I assume that self-expression involves self-government, and that we ought to aim not merely at giving people votes, but at calling forth their full participation in the common direction of the affairs of the community.' Other guild socialist advocates were to put forward practical proposals for the reconstruction of the trade union movement on a syndicalist and federalist basis – such as Orage and S.G. Hobson in their series of articles on National Guilds in 1912-13 and by Bechhofer and Reckitt in their 1917 book *The Meaning of National Guilds*. In practice the guild socialist movement soon became swamped by the growth of national unions such as Ernest Bevin's Transport and General Workers Unions. One of the failures of the movement was to make the link to the growing political municipal labour movement, as Labour in the post-war period won control of significant cities across the country.

On the continent, a group of German left radicals advocated an approach to workers organization that became known as council communism. The leading advocate was the Dutch astronomer Anton Pannekoek, who moved from Leyden to the German S.P.D. party college in Berlin, and then to Bremen. It was not until after the war that Pannekoek, who had joined the German communist party, was to advocate in his articles on 'Workers Councils' workplace organisations as the basic political units of the class struggle. He drew a contrast with state socialism, seen as preserving the basic fabric of capitalism. He also contrasted workers councils with parliamentarism. To Pannekoek, 'the collaborating workers, having common interests and belonging together in the praxis of daily life, can send some real representatives and spokesmen. Complete democracy is realized here in the equal rights of everyone who takes part in the work.' The fundamental principle of council communism was a belief in independent working class action. Some of the approaches of the council communists were later shared by Otto Ruhle, one time colleague of Rosa Luxemburg and Karl Leibknecht in the Spartacist movement. Luxemburg had advocated the General Strike in 1905 and later in 1917-18, only to be regarded by Lenin as an ultra-leftist. Ruhle was to take Pannekoek's belief in workplace organization and the primacy of economic organization to argue against the very existence of working class-based political parties, as only workplace-based organisations could avoid the authoritarianism and centralism that was endemic in a political organization. Similar arguments for proletarian self-determination were put forward by German communist Karl Korsch. Approaching the issue from a philosophical perspective, Korsch developed a legal framework for factory councils, and argued that factory councils should be the basis for the socialization of the economy: the bringing of the fundamental structures of capitalism under workers control. Korsch's activity was not limited to theory. In 1918 he was a member of the Socialisation Commission established to advice the post-war socialist German government, a group which also included Karl Kautsky and Rudolf Hilferding and the economist Joseph Shumpeter. While the Commission was unable to impose national programme in a post-war context of economic collapse and political instability, it did give some support to local initiatives, such as the socialization of the mines in the Ruhr by local workers and soldiers councils. Elements of libertarian socialist traditions can also be found in the writings and political practice of the Austro-Marxists of the 1920s and early 1930s. Karl Renner saw the council system as the basis of both working class power and democracy. Before the First World War the Austrian socialists had supported both decentralized political structures and the rights of nationalities within the collapsing Austro-Hungarian empire. In the post-war period, Austrian socialists such as Max Adler, Otto Bauer and Rudolf Hilferding all sought to reintroduce ethics into what remained a Marxist-based socialist movement, a movement that, in establishing the Vienna based Two-and-a-half International, sought to act as a bridge between social reformism and communism and which also established in the city of Vienna an advanced municipal socialism providing a high quality of collectively managed services to the working class population, but a political power base not strong enough to resist fascism in 1934.

As the competition between communism and fascism grew, it was more difficult for independent socialists to have an influence beyond localities. The exception was perhaps in Spain, where as well as a strong anarcho-syndicalist movement and a developed tradition of both urban and rural collectives, there was a strong libertarian socialist political movement in the Barcelona based P.O.U.M. made famous by George Orwells' *Homage to Catalonia*, inheritors of the tradition of Pi y Margall's Catalan federalists of the 1870s but suppressed by both the Communist Party and then by the Francoists. After the Second World War, the tradition becomes even weaker, emerging only in the anti-authoritarian nationalist communism of Imre Nagy in Hungary in 1956 and Dubcek in Czechoslovakia in 1968 – movements more effectively revolts against Soviet domination than arguments for workers control and decentralization within the national states. More positive was the development of economic self-management in Tito's Yugoslavia. 1968 in Paris, meanwhile, while providing some opportunities for workers' self-management, was primarily a revolt against the authoritarian Gaullist state rather than a positive argument for more decentralized forms of government. 1968 was after all more a revolt of student intellectuals.

Already a privileged class led primarily by ultra-left groupuscules rather than a proletarian-based movement for independent working class autonomy. Nevertheless in the post-1968 movement, there were elements within what became a very disparate socialist movement advocating forms of autonomous working class political and economic leadership: what became known as 'autogestion', advocated by politicians such as Michel Rocard and Jean-Pierre Chevenement and economists such as Jacques Attali.

This leads us on to the state of libertarian socialism in the British labour movement in the last twenty years. While in the 1980s there was a short burst of municipal socialism, mainly in defence of local Labour Party power against the Thatcherite government, just as there was a limited revival of union militancy, these were largely defensive rather than positive events. Attempts to create new forms of decentralized political and economic power seeking to achieve socialist transformations predicated on commitments to both democracy and equality were few and far between. Sparks of light in this otherwise bleak landscape include the work of the Nottingham-based Institute of Workers Control, the early Labour Co-ordination Committee, the Lucas Aerospace Combine, Rowbotham, Wainwright and Segal's *Beyond the Fragments* (1979), Geoff Hodgson's *The Democratic Economy* (1984), Mike Rustin's *For a Pluralist Socialism* (1985), Peter Hain's *Radical Regeneration* (1975), Michael Meacher's *Socialism with a Human Face* (1982) and Diffusing Power (1992), and Chartist's own *New Maps for the Nineties* of 1990. More recently there is the advocacy of 'deepening democracy' drawing inspiration from the municipal social initiatives and participatory democracy in Porto Alegre in Brazil, and new groups such as London Citizens who are seeking to develop local political self-empowerment, in contrast to the essentially oppositionist and protest based agitation of the anti-globalisation movement.

In the Labour Party at national level, political splits and differences related more to personalities than principles. Even the internal battles of the 1980s were more about control of the party than a real debate over the party's objectives – never mind the issues of how a real and lasting tradition to socialism was achieved. Instead we have achieved not just a transition to Thatcherism but a transition to a form of corporate and market power which is beyond a political process, a disempowerment of workplace organization and a complete disempowerment of local government structures as even basic welfare state services are privatized or run on the basis of private sponsorship. Basic libertarian socialist principles of collective management, and the active political engagement in management of a public sector at a range of levels are regarded, so far as they are even mentioned, not just as historical anachronisms but as some form of naïve utopianism that has no relevance to contemporary realities. We are now in a political party that not only has no socialist principle but has lost any knowledge of its own history or why it was created. Only through understanding where we started have we any chance of moving forward.

Beyond Blair 88 Far from one-trick

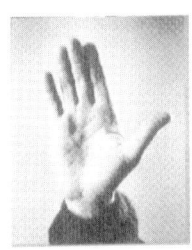 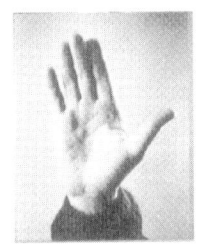 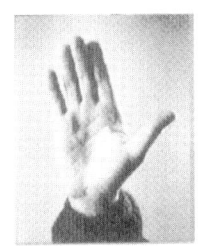

Section 3: Review

1990 seems such a long time ago. But is it really? Yes, the internet was an apple in a computer scientist's eye back then, and the Arctic Monkeys may have been in pre-school, but these are superficial.

Who could have foreseen that such liberal right-wing policies as free-market permeation of public services or the refusal to take a misfiring privatised sector back into public hands would have been enacted and entrenched by a 'socialist' government? Sixteen years ago, a group of writers clustered around the leftist publication *Chartist* attempted to map out a future for socialism. But did their 'Third Road' reflect the 'Third Way' that became ideological dogma for New Labour?

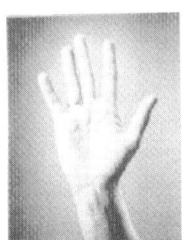 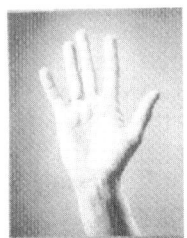 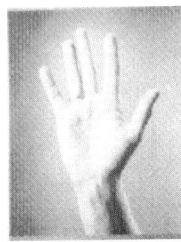

Navigating the 'Third Road':

How accurate were the New Maps?

Martin Cook

More than fifteen years have passed since *Chartist's* writers tackled the problems facing the future of socialism. In that time much water has flowed under the bridge. The collapse of the Soviet bloc, already under way in 1990, has now largely been accomplished with generally unpleasant results. While Thatcher and Reagan are mercifully no longer on the scene, the have been replaced by politicians of the right, 'left' and centre whose politics represent either a continuation of their free market deregulatory polices (as with Clinton, Bush jr and Blair) or at best a gradual accommodation to them (Jospin, Schroeder and co.). Despite the general lack of enthusiasm for these job destroying and livelihood cutting policies there have only been sporadic protests so far. In the last decades, the 1995 revolt against Juppé's austerity package in France and the anti-globalisation movement's successes from Seattle to Cancun, via Porto Alegre and Genoa, have been encouraging signs of progressive revival, especially among radical youth.

Global capitalism stands indicted on many scores. Especially since the 1980s, growth rates have been feeble compared to the post-war glory days (1945-74). Worse than this, the distribution of wealth rapidly worsened in tune with the move away from Keynesianism, state intervention and 'welfare collectivism' across the west. This was especially true in the U.S.A., where organized labour was weak and poorly placed to fight back. Moreover, even the modest moves towards development in the poor quarters of the world largely stalled after the 1970s as they were dragooned into following free market nostrums with even more dismal effects. There have been exceptions in China and the 'Asian dragons', but based on forced state-led development rather than the pure marketism of the so-called 'Washington consensus'. The desperate ecological problems created by modern capitalism are further items on the charge sheet, not to mention the vicious ethnic and religious clashes often worsened by backwardness and economic regression.

In the circumstances, and especially with the decline of the dead hand of old guard 'Communism' (i.e. Stalinism), you might think that at last the conditions were in place for a global revival of a newly confident socialist left. However, the most effective movements have generally been of a 'non-party' basis, and have suffered from the inability to go beyond protest and critique to positive solutions and practical advance. It is not, as is said, that the new movements lack coherence or considered alternatives – they have these aplenty, from practical immediate reforms to radical global alternatives. What they lack are organizational forms and credible political projects – which implies, realistically, parties and programmes of whatever type.

I believe that if we look afresh at the ideas in *Chartist*'s *New Maps for the Nineties* of 1990, then we can easily see why the left as a whole, from the most pragmatic to the 'fundamentalists', has been unable to respond to the new challenges and opportunities of the 1990s and 2000s.

Although *Chartist* comrades produced much of the document, it was co-sponsored by the Clause IV grouping. This was a network set up in 1974 to provide a 'broad left' type alternative to the sectarian antics of groups like 'Militant' in the Labour Party. Over the years, it debated sophisticated critiques of capitalism and old-guard socialism, in which we joined them. However, they dissolved shortly after this time because they had 'won' – presumably with the dispersal of the trots and the marginalization of the 'hard left', certainly not with a resurgence of left politics in general! Since then some Clause IV members have become M.Ps and cabinet ministers under 'New Labour' (Denham, Hain, Clarke) while others have remained more independent and come out against Blairism.

Trevor Fisher: Introduction

Back in 1980 Trevor wrote in *Chartist* a rather pessimistic piece suggesting that a revival of the left and of Labour after Thatcher's initial victory was not to be counted on, and his jeremiads have often been vindicated since. In his introduction, he briefly outlined the purpose of 'Third Road' politics as a progressive alternative to the dead ends of traditional state led parliamentary reformism and of Leninist 'insurrectionism'.

As he put it:
'It is widely believed on the British left that this situation is down

to a crisis of leadership, notably that of the Labour Party and the T.U.C. A crisis of leadership there certainly is. However, there is also a crisis of the rank and file, and a crisis of theory and a lack of intellectual confidence. It is time to face up to the realities of the dilemmas, contradictions and weaknesses of the British left.'

There we have it in a nutshell. As he says, who back in the 1970s could have imagined the Tories could do what they did without effective opposition?

Fisher disposes easily enough of the delusions of the established left. He notes the absurd illusion that radical social and economic changes can take place on a purely parliamentary basis without a strong extra-parliamentary wing to generate popular support for socialism. The lack of a strong popular base for left politics ensures what he calls 'accommodation to the centre', and he predicts a Labour government might do no better than 'manage the system' within the parameters set by Thatcherism. Sixteen years on, even the latter seems optimistic as 'New Labour' in many ways has sought to entrench and extend Thatcherism, not merely accommodate to it.

Fisher's treatment of the far-left is more questionable. In the first place, he dubs them 'insurrectionists'. Let's face it, there have been 'Leninist' type groups in the U.K. since just after 1917, and there has hardly been an occasion when any of them did any serious work of an insurrectionary kind. The latter would imply a systematic policy of infiltration of the armed forces, or else forming some private guerrilla army. In practice, what the revolutionary or semi-revolutionary sects have done is to campaign for immediate reforms and against various governments at the same time as effectively saying to supporters 'anything achievable under capitalism isn't really worth having'. There has been a contradiction between revolutionary ideologies and the situation around them, which they try to pretend away by denouncing other sects as having sold the pass under bourgeois pressure.

Fisher is also wrong to say the far-left sees nothing problematic in either working-class consciousness or socialism itself. This really only describes the crudest Gerry-Healy-on-a-bad-night Trotskyist ranter. This is important because, as and when democratic socialists enter into debate with the sectarian fringe, we need to have a clear idea of what they do stand for. Many pages of their discussion magazines are, in fact, devoted to issues of class-consciousness and reformist 'illusions' or to dealing with the contamination of the socialist 'brand' by Soviet or Fabian type bureaucracies. In fact, these groups have often involved sophisticated intellectuals such as Cliff Slaughter, Tom Kemp, Robin Blackburn and Lynn Walsh – let alone the likes of Hobsbawm in the old Communist Party.

Where he is spot on is on the extent to which the far-left (and the 'hard left' influenced by it) have failed to note the decline not only in overt socialist awareness but also in basic class-consciousness as such since the middle twentieth century. Similarly wide doubts on the virtues of centralized and top-down so-called 'socialism' cannot be shrugged off by blaming it all on Stalin or whoever. To what extent one should denounce 'statist' socialism per se is a complex issue to which we will return.

Trevor next outlines the basics of a 'Third Road' approach (alias 'soft left', strategic or 'libertarian'). This itself is problematic since so many of those once associated with the soft left or Gramscian approaches – whether ex-Communists like Mulgan or Leadbetter or Labour Coordinating Committee luminaries like many recent New Labour apparatchiks – have either abandoned this stance or were using it as a cover to attack orthodox leftism from the right. This is a point Trevor makes in the original 1990 document, well borne out by time. The Third Road derived from the best parts of the likes of Gramsci and Poulantzas; that we should neither see the state as a neutral arbiter nor entertain simplistic ideas of 'smashing' it. Gramscian ideas can be used to outline a strategy of working 'in and against the state' - a popular 1980s phrase - strengthening the progressive forces within in it rather than taking it on in open combat. This fits in with Gramsci's ideas on the need to counter the 'hegemony' used by the ruling class to dominate us by our own socialist hegemony – though whether the Italian communist leader actually broke with Lenin on these issues is debatable. As Trevor puts it, any concept of 'the end justifies the means' has to go. Desirable outcomes of whatever sort must be 'built into the political process', not something to be bolted on at some unspecified date in the future. Our movement must be democratic, open and participatory in the here and now – not in some future Golden Age. Thus, he is quite right to say the Third Road cannot just be some compromise between left reformism and 'Leninism' but must go beyond both. Socialism can only be won with the active participation of working people in the struggle.

Trevor's initial conclusion was that the road forward was to take these 'Third Road' democratic socialist politics into the Labour Party: something that now seems less plausible than ever. On the positive side, however, the years since 1990 have seen the increasing decline and marginalization of both the old left-reform and Bolshevik movements in this country and beyond. If the S.W.P. or whoever sometimes looks likes a credible force, it is only because it operates in a political vacuum. Meanwhile Trevor berates the 'Bennite' left (Campaign Group etc) for its 'oppositionalism' (sic).

However, this phrase is nowadays used by apologists for 'New Labour' to slate opponents of their neo-Thatcherite course. Obviously, it's better to be fighting for a progressive alternative to the status quo, but opposing mindlessly may be better than not opposing attacks on our social gains and living standards at all!

1. Paul Thomposon on 'Transition'

Paul Thompson's piece is rich and dense, covering many of the key issues of debate for modern socialists. He begins by demolishing the great 'revolution vs. reform' or 'parliament vs. extra parliamentary' dichotomies. As he stresses, in practice most left reformists are prepared to use extra-parliamentary pressure or movements from time to time, just as 'revolutionaries' spend a lot of time campaigning for reforms or getting elected to parliaments. The real divide, he suggests, should be based on socialist goals as opposed to the tactics and strategy for getting there.

Paul's central argument is that our model of socialism should be a pluralist one – as opposed to the centrally 'planned' command economy of the former U.S.S.R., for example. This would mean both pluralism in a political sense – with checks and balances – and a state that enabled more than controlled in the economic sphere. Rather than one-size-fits-all, one would have a range of enterprises (public, private, co-operative or democratically managed) operating in a form of market socialist economy. Planning would exist however, and be extended down to localities plus up to the international level. Political pluralism may seem obvious, but even in the 1980s there was a kind of 'Labour Leninism': the idea one party would somehow, through its network of committees and conferences, capture the state, and then ram its left programme down the throat of everybody else. The idea that we want to decentralize decision-making down to local communities and recognize diverse interests, even if that means we do not always get our way, is an important insight. He is right to query ideas of a 'fixed and finished' socialism, if anyone held them – Marx certainly saw future society as endlessly fluid.

Like other *New Maps* writers, Paul begs a number of key issues. One of these is the purported declining size of the working class. He seems to base himself on theorists like Poulantzas who start from the proposition of rejecting the 'obvious' idea that those who go out and work for someone else for living are, broadly, the working class. If the workers are declining, it is because the 'intermediate strata' are growing in size. Now, who exactly are these people? Overwhelmingly, in the real world, they are technical, financial, clerical or professional employees – civil servants, supervisors, shop workers, teaching and medical staff, and computer boffins... For Marx, the key issue in society was the way the social surplus is 'pumped out' from the immediate producers by those who control the means of creating wealth. Implicitly, Paul must regard the 'immediate producers' as being alternatively, manual workers, private sector workers, those producing profit/ surplus, or those without higher education.

It is obvious that an awful lot of folk are low income, low status employees with little stake in the system and few rights: supermarket staff, call-centre prisoners, classroom assistants, basic-grade teachers, nurses, waiters, bar staff etc. True, some staff are in constant demand and can easily move to better jobs if they are badly treated and thus feel little need for a union – accountants, project managers, lawyers, property professionals and so on; but is this true for most librarians, social workers or fitness centre employees? Put it another way, these days most trade unions – including mine – are a mixture of employees at all levels. Are we trying to represent sections of the population with conflicting interests? Closer to home, who does the left itself comprise? Overwhelmingly it is these same intermediate professional or semi-professional groups – typically public sector teachers, social workers and civil servants. Does the modern left represent the 'special interests' of such groups, as opposed to those of horny-handed sons of toil (clever Tory apologists would no doubt say so!)? From a Marxian point of view being a 'productive worker' (i.e. producing profit/ surplus value) might be the key category. But if the state takes railways, water or health services into public ownership again will these staff exit the proletariat?

We are not talking about abstract sociological debate here. If I remain broadly optimistic about socialist progress, it is because I consider socialism is a movement in the interests of the overwhelming majority of the human race (an increasing one in fact), not just some beleaguered minority of the socially excluded or unskilled labourers. The organized core of leftist movements has always tended to be the better off and more educated and skilled sections – skilled engineering workers in 1900, maybe computer workers, planners or teachers today! For Paul it is necessary for labour to be constantly building alliances with other social groupings with (implicitly) conflicting interests, a rather debilitating prospect. To me, these alliances are best seen as resolving differences within a broad diverse modern proletariat – who are common victims of being shafted by the wealthy elite as pension schemes are looted, public services run down and conditions degraded.

Paul moves on to the critique of the 'Leninist' position, whereby the state as a whole is 'smashed' and replaced by a new state of workers' councils (something that has never happened anywhere). He stresses the need for a hegemonic movement to win support or acquiescence in socialist transition from currently reactionary sections of society, via a strategy of radical reforms and forcing the state to respond increasingly to popular pressures. As he points out, complex modern society needs the state to intervene in society in all sorts of ways, notably the welfare state including the N.H.S., for instance – whatever the original intentions, this cannot simply be a means of propping up capitalism but allows the development of services based on human needs not just profit. Thatcher and Major hardly reduced the size of state activity in nearly two decades.

When Paul suggests that not classes but parties actually wield state power one has to say "up to a point, Lord Copper." Is it really the case that a mere shift in governing party changes something real in the state? Only in extreme circumstances. Mostly, leftist parties have exercised power in the context of running the system on lines perfectly acceptable to the ruling class, if not preferable to blinkered right wing parties – significantly, the *Financial Times* came out for a Labour vote even under Kinnock in 1992. It is true that the 'working class' did not seize power in 1917 – a vanguard party based on it did, which rapidly suppressed all forms of democratic control so that that class could in no way be said to exercise power. What is true, however, is that any party that does exercise power does so on the basis of support from some class force or other – in the case of New Labour for instance, a precarious combination of forces. A political party with no significant 'class' base will win few elections, if any. Paul prefers a Poulantzas type 'revisionist' account of politics whereas I suggest that Ralph Miliband's more orthodox reading of Marxism has more to tell us. Recent history suggests that Marxists were right in stressing the dominance of the capitalist elite in society.

Paul concludes with accounts of how leftist governments in Sweden and Austria have managed to advanced working class interests within the existing framework. His points are fair enough in part, still there is little evidence that these projects ever seriously jeopardized the capitalist status quo. Sadly enough, sixteen years on, these projects have succumbed in many ways to neo-liberalism and right wing populism even if not to the extent of the collapse of social democracy in Britain. He also adds in a piece on Allende in Chile, suggesting that a more subtle approach to centre and right wing forces could possibly have staved off disaster and resisted the coup - a typical 'eurocommunist' account, but none the worse for that.

2. Don Flynn on 'Reformism'

Analysis of reform socialism or social democracy has often been from 'orthodox' leftists who castigate it for selling out the masses and assume that any crumbs achieved under capitalism by working people really can't be worth having. Conversely, there are histories from within the reformist trend that are entirely uncritical and take it for granted that a few marginal improvements in the status quo are all that one could reasonably hope for. Don Flynn's excellent paper on this subject is a pragmatic and realistic account, in a Marxian framework, which deals sympathetically with the phenomenon. It suggests that within British 'Labourism' gradualism and parliamentarism cannot be attributed to a backward political culture or to a thin crust of reactionary labour aristocrats/right wing bureaucrats holding back the potentially revolutionary rank and file.

Don suggests that the origins of reformism stem from the very nature of building a mass workers' movement in the classical capitalism of the late nineteenth century. Inevitably, the new parties' supporters wanted answers to practical immediate concerns: education, health, housing and the like. In this sense the German 'revisionist' Bernstein was reflecting the demands of the time rather than the more left or centre Marxist 'orthodoxy' of Rosa Luxemburg or Karl Kautsky. Attempts by radical revolutionaries to set up new 'pure' socialist or communist movements before and after the First World War could only be negative, splitting the effective unity of a broad proletarian movement. Reformism was realistic because western capitalism, except for a fairly brief period in the inter-war years, was always able to offer substantial reform benefits in the form of worker rights, the welfare state, pensions and greater democratic possibilities.

Having said this, Don repeats the basic error of Paul Thompson by stating, as if it were obvious, that the working class, far from becoming the overwhelming majority of the population, has always and everywhere remained a minority even in the most advanced and industrialized western societies. While he does not specify what 'orthodox' definition he is working on, he states that the children of factory workers often went off to work in shops and offices. Flynn argues that the likes of Bernstein recognized this new reality and thus called for alliances with wider social groups, unlike old guard Marxists who refused to accept these changes. Leninist vanguardism is thus seen as a way of short-circuiting the problem of socialism no longer being a movement of the majority.

As argued above, I do not accept this limited definition of the working class and I doubt that Marx would have done either. Like many others, Don attacks a 'straw man' caricature of a proletariat increasingly levelled and homogenized in terms of its subjective experience in the massive factories of the 1880-1930 period. I could point out that in 1900 there was a massive split in the allegedly homogenous British working class between church and chapel, Liberal and Tory. Electoral victories by leftist parties have often been rather larger in the later twentieth century as wider sections of the so called 'middle class' became radicalized and unionized, and the passing of generations removed the inertia of right wing politics (even now, many working class pensioners are folk who grew up in the 1920s and 1930s when Labour was still a small minority outside the areas of heavy industry). The problem was the slow progress of left politics even within the 'core' manual proletariat. Not till 1945 did Labour get a majority of 'blue collar' votes, at a time when they comprised eighty per cent of the population.

Don is right to stress the role of the trade unions in British 'Labourism' and to a lesser extent continental reformism. He notes the inevitably sectional role that unions have in promoting the interests of a particular group, whether male workers, the skilled or whoever. At the end of the day they wouldn't be much use if they failed to do this! As he says, unions are 'self-interested operators within the labour market'. This means they inevitably have to be decentralized and it is hard for a leftist party seeking to carry out progressive reforms to get a consensus on measures that may not enhance the short-term position of some constituencies. Don accounts for the flexible nature of reformism in the need to take account of the different and often competing demands of particular groups. It is clear that this means the unions never had much time for 'fundamentalist' all-or-nothing versions of socialist politics. Unions are an essential basis for a socialist project, but that cannot be just 'the T.U.C. writ large'. Having said this, we can see how the broad mass of unions over the last 150 years moved from being mainly uncritical supporters of capitalist society in the 1850s to predominantly radical critics. Unison, the T.G.W.U. and the G.M.W.U. may not be dominated by the Communist Party or 'Trots' but they endorse many or most of the critiques of the anti-globalization movement of recent years. Outright Blairites are utterly marginalized in most unions, who see what their neo-Thatcherism means in practice.

Don goes on to stress the basis for modern reformism in the Keynesian full employment settlement post-1945 with the ideology of post capitalism, developed by Anthony Crosland et al. The collapse of the post-war consensus and its ideology of compromise led to the revival of an atavistic syndicalist revival around the 1970s, epitomized by Arthur Scargill. This offered no realistic hegemonic way forward and duly collapsed in defeat, despite the sophisticated ideas generated around the Alternative Economic Strategy.

Don concludes that traditional reformism is vitiated for the future by its class emphasis (this I question), its workplace orientation, its 'statism', its exclusively parliamentary approach and its 'narrow nationalism'. Moreover, reformism was dominated by relatively 'conservative' interests within the working class bloc. In so far as this criticism was valid, the last twenty-five years have seen radical change among what remains of 'reformism' in the unions and beyond. These criticisms relate to a model which socialists like ourselves encountered in the early 1970s but has largely passed away in the early twenty-first century. Looking to the future, Don quotes Gramsci's distinction of 'hard' and 'soft' reformism, i.e. radical change of the national culture vs. tepid amelioration of conditions. This is akin to the arguments of the late Ralph Miliband for a radical left reformism as the most plausible vehicle of modern socialism.

Where Don errs is in suggesting that the Marxian approach is wrong per se. If you read G.A. Cohen's book Karl Marx's *Theory of History* for example, you will finds it is intellectually valid and defensible. Where too many modern Marxists go wrong, however, is in ignoring the limits to this core analysis. Marx placed too much value on the free market schemas of Smith and Ricardo and seems to have believed that this represented capitalist reality. In the real world, capitalism has existed only in historical social formations. If anyone actually tried to implement a 'pure' free market world it would all collapse around their ears as we see in countries like Argentina today. Naturally, as Don very well points out, these measures of reform, compromise and integration of working people – especially their better-off strata – laid the basis for reform politics. Socialism needs to be aware that modern-day capitalism really is about greedy bustards in top hats grinding their boots in the faces of the workers like a 1970s agit-prop skit. But it is also about far far more - hence the complexity of our task.

3. Trevor Fisher on 'Leninism'

You might wonder why, even in 1990, folk like us were bothering with the Bolshevik legacy. What possible relevance could the tactics and policies of underground revolutionaries in Czarist Russia before the First World War have for the left in modern Western Europe? The answer is that, sadly, the influence of the neo-Leninists in the 1970s/80s ran far beyond its tiny numbers. From the 1920s to the late 1960s the British left, even the Labour left, had been dominated by the politics of the Communist Party of Great Britain. These politics had rarely been ultra left except in the notorious 'Third Period' (1928-32) and often C.P.-ers were the most sensible folk in a local union branch or such-like. They had a moderate strategic reform policy despite their ideological hang-ups about the dear old U.S.S.R. From the late 1960s this hold was challenged by the rise of an angry and impatient 'new left' of ex-students, often working in the public sector as teachers or social workers for instance – this paralleling the decline of the old heavy industries. By the 1980s many of these comrades had got involved in the Labour Party itself, either in organized groups like the erstwhile Militant - now the 'Socialist Party' - or as unaffiliated individuals.

As Trevor points out superbly, the influence of these groups was almost wholly negative, whether in the Labour Party or any other campaigns. That is not to deny their immense hard work and effectiveness from time to time in building mass campaigns such as the Anti-Nazi League (run by the Socialist Workers Party). As he puts it, 'Leninism was from the outset sectarian, authoritarian and anti-democratic' (for chapter and verse see Robin Blick's pamphlet *The Seeds of Evil*). He quotes 1930s writer Storm Jameson in explaining the appeal of the hyper-activism (marches, demos, paper sales, rallies...) that motivates the endlessly recycled group of activists to keep going; many found this a pleasant contrast to the tedious routine and electoral obsessions of the Labour Party.

Trevor notes the paradox that Trotskyists attack New Labour or capitalism for their authoritarianism when in most cases they run their internal regimes as mini police states. The leadership always seems to be right however often the line changes, and the 'party' has a monopoly of wisdom compared to even all the other sects who are revisionists, centrists or what have you. Internal opponents are disloyal, petty bourgeois (i.e. 'middle class'), inactive and so on. As Sheila Rowbotham said, if the S.W.P. (ex-International Socialists) became so authoritarian in the mid 1970s in Britain, imagine what it would be like in a situation of revolution or civil war! One small recent example was in the Birmingham S.W.P. when critical local members were told not to e-mail each other with their views by the local organizer. Imagine what Socialist Worker would say if such restrictions were enforced by employers or union leaderships!

As Trevor says, the disorganization and lack of theory of the mainstream Labour left made it easy for the sects to gain disproportionate influence for many years especially in localities like Liverpool and in the party youth movement (L.P.Y.S). Their approach was based on a simple-minded view of Marxism, which takes the basic facts of capitalist oppression as the be-all and end-all. As argued above, real life capitalism grew up in particular societies at particular times. Class struggle from below was met by reform and compromise from above. Parliamentary reform was not just a glorified con trick, and Marx's own ultra-leftist prognosis on the uselessness of parliaments was not borne out. As Don Flynn showed, this created the growth of the European reformist tradition that Lenin and Trotsky reacted against (rightly denouncing the support of many though by no means all social democrats for the First World War).

As Trevor continues, beyond their immediate impact Leninist sects intensified all-or-nothing politics or 'oppositionalism' – anything that can be achieved in the here and now is a 'sell-out' – and permanent factional opposition to the leadership even when the latter are broad-left activists in a local party or union branch. Failures can all be written off as 'betrayals of the leadership' which may in some cases be true but explains nothing in the long run (as Engels pointed out long ago). While Trevor is broadly right here, it is true that social democrat reformist leaders can sometimes be more effective at carrying out right-wing policies than an open right-wing government, and also that union leaders – when workers are in a strong position – often play the role of a 'fire brigade' rather than extracting maximum gains.

The fact that what the far-left says has a certain congruence with reality explains their appeal. They are not just like Jehovah's Witnesses constantly prophesying doom and destruction, though they do this as well! One point they make that Trevor skates over is the fact – pointed out a hundred years back by Michels and Ostrogorski – that socialist and union bureaucrats who do politics as a day job do have a vested interest that often differs from the rest of us. They want a quiet life, deals with employers or the Tories. Their career prospects are often enhanced by doing what the union or party hierarchy wants; not by responding to the rank and files' needs. Since 1994, we have seen numerous ex-radicals succumb to the blandishments of being M.Ps, M.E.Ps, council cabinet members or health authority members – often at lucrative salaries. What the Trots will not tell you is that the same applies in spades to themselves. If you vote out the leadership of the S.W.P. you may be depriving certain full time organizers of their jobs. Leading on from this it is remarkable how often an eccentric theory is only perpetuated by being the emblem or fetish of a sect. Other than the S.W.P. and its co-thinkers abroad, who in the real world thinks the U.S.S.R. was a form of capitalism?

Trevor's best point is about this leadership obsession. Within the Labour Party, many non-Trotskyists such as the Campaign For Labour Party Democracy and the Campaign Group have had a policy that stresses winning motions at local or national meetings, rule changes, and replacing 'right' leaders with 'left' ones. None of this is wrong in itself, but it ignores the fact that these things are determined by the overall balance of forces in society – class struggle and all the ideology/cultural stuff that goes with it. If society is heading to the right because our side is losing, then the best 'left' leaders will fail or rapidly move to the right themselves. We have enough evidence of the latter in recent years!

Fundamentally, Trevor concludes, the idea that in societies saturated with decades of struggles to enhance parliamentary democracy, the left can proceed by 'insurrectionary' means against parliament and violent overthrow of the existing state machinery looks highly implausible. It was daft enough even in 1921 when the old Communist Party was set up. The authoritarian regimes of vanguard parties are bad enough before a revolution, let alone afterwards. Yet they cannot be ignored – without a coherent critique and alternative, these sects will revive again with any new upsurge in socialist activity as they did in the 1960s/70s. The fact that Militant and their like left the party in the 1980s will not stop them intervening in the future, in however destabilizing a way, as some of the micro-sects still do.

4. Paul Hoggett on 'Local socialism'

During the 1980s, *Chartist* placed a lot of stress on a 'pre-figurative' approach to socialism – the idea that socialist politics should not just involve describing a distant future, but be involved in practice in the day-to-day activities the left engages in. If we could not achieve much on the national stage where Thatcher reigned supreme, there were still numerous local authorities, especially in London, where left Labour had come to power around 1980. These experiences are of course particularly British yet should hold some interest for comrades abroad where local government often has more power and independence than in this country. Paul Hoggett's tour d'horizon casts a positive but deservedly sceptical eye over this experience, which seems rather ancient history given the recent centralizing 'control-freakery' of New Labour.

This was an opportunity to put into practice the ideas of 'In and Against the State' as argued by critical leftists in the early 1980s. The state at a local level could be considered as a site for progressive struggle against capitalism, even if in the past it had been involved in practices that helped control or subjugate the population. Radical critiques of social work, policing, housing policy, education and town planning were brought to bear by newly arrived and often naïve leftists who found themselves chairing council committees who spent hundreds of millions a year with workforces of many thousands. Thus, this was not simply about using the local state but developing alliances with bodies in what became known as civil society – tenants, women's groups, ethnic minorities and environmentalists.

Paul's approach is refreshing if controversial. He embodies a strong libertarian strain from the 1980s *Chartist*, stressing that 'Within civil society we react against the state and the economy but we also seek to reproduce ourselves as imaginative, sensitive and transformative beings, albeit within the constraints set by the pincers of the state, the workplace and the market.' He is right to stress that all-or-nothing socialists who believe in 'no responsibility under capitalism' have no business being involved in running local government. Unfortunately, as we saw in Liverpool and elsewhere, some of the new local left had semi-Trotskyist politics and saw the experience as a death or glory attempt to take on Thatcherism using gesture politics that culminated in going bankrupt by not setting a legal rate.

The best local socialists had a more subtle view that saw the contradictory nature of the modern welfare state for capitalism – on the one hand it was necessary to perform essential functions (education, health care, social work, care homes etc) which free enterprise did not want, but it deprived the market of potential profit making areas and constituted gains won by organized labour after 1945. As Paul says, local socialism is a core part of a strategic concept of socialist reform to be achieved over decades or more – not by some millennial 'big bang' a-la 1917.

One of the many difficulties is that the state is in the business of managing need not satisfying it – and local councils lack the resources to increase massively such facilities as housing repairs or nurseries. Paul is critical of 'technocratic' professions such as town planners, social workers, teachers and the like – who can be seen as pursuing self-interested agendas with the help of their trade unions, at the same time as patronizing and marginalizing the ordinary residents who pay their salaries. There may be some truth in this but I am not convinced that professionalization must be a bad thing. Modern society and individual needs are very complex and subtle – is it a bad thing if staff are trained for some years to get a deeper understanding of the conditions they have to grapple with?

Paul also raises the issue of representative democracy: the professional cadre of local councillors elected on a party ticket, often for national reasons, who achieve a monopoly of power on most decisions despite occasional nods to decentralization. His answer is to transfer funding and power away from these professional and political hierarchies to the 'self-organized' local groups. This sounds all very fine in principle, but anyone involved in local community politics knows the limited pool of talent to get involved in such things even when successful.

Whatever you say about local authorities and other traditional bodies like trade unions and political parties, and how they may be dominated by 'unrepresentative activists' they are usually transparent, open and accountable, operating in a legal framework. If councillors or officers are corrupt it is easy for the Audit Commission to sort them out; similarly national parties and unions can sort out local branches taken over by head-bangers of some kind. In the sordid world of everyday life, it is easy for more informal bodies to be set up – or taken over – by opportunists with corrupt or cynical agendas posing as so-called 'community leaders'. It is thought that large amounts of public money were given to such worthless bodies by the old G.L.C. in the latter years of its existence.

My colleagues in the authority I work in spend a great deal of time monitoring and checking the way public funds are spent by bodies funded out of council tax payers' pockets. In some cases monitoring may cost nearly as much as the grant, but if the public finds out money has been squandered on high living or Swiss bank accounts it is 'local socialism' that will be discredited. This applies just as much to the possibilities of internal corruption and instances of waste, skiving and restrictive practices in the public sector locally. Where this has been endemic long-term it has besmirched the reputations of the left, local government and the trade union movement.

None of this negates Paul's arguments for the state to transfer funding and powers to responsible community-led groups, but the situation is more problematic than he suggests. Furthermore local government itself has got far more sophisticated at client surveys, equality work, community development and the like since the 1980s. Folk want basic services delivered, and at least councillors and their managers have to be available to deal with issues raised for fear of the Ombudsman! When control is outsourced whether to private companies or to 'community-led' groups, placing responsibility for mistakes or securing changes in services may not be easier to achieve.

The decentralization of functions to local offices has made great progress in many areas and is usually welcomed by those affected (council housing for instance). Nonetheless, it may involve expensive duplication of staffing if taken too far, and usually it is matter of administration rather than policy. As many sceptics have suggested, do we really want a position where the availability of decent schools, libraries, parks or day centres depends on the quirks of local communities and activists? Voters and community groups in well-heeled areas may choose to cut or abolish services to the less fortunate of the kind they do not use personally, as we see in Wandsworth. I also wonder about making top local government officers political appointees. Within local councils it is often suggested that managers spend too much trying to please their political masters as opposed to pleasing the clients or getting on with the job, even with a supposedly non-political set-up. The conversion of being a senior councillor into a full-time job has not meant an infusion of more working class representatives as Paul hoped, but more a rush to the gravy train by careerist politicos.

When Paul moves on to the tendentious equality area his vision is, I think, impaired by the idea that the only problems are those of entrenched prejudice among local hierarchies of elderly white males. This is a caricature of how things were twenty-five years ago. In the period since there are now many councils in which ethnic minorities, women and other under-represented groups have become increasingly visible at councillor and manager level. Authorities have gone to great lengths to ensure that workforces and client groups represent local communities, but this is not a simple issue. Councils recruit from all over Britain, all over the world. If twenty-five percent of the population of a borough are Bangladeshis, does this have to be represented in every single department or section? In town planning we now have a mainly female workforce among younger staff because men prefer the more lucrative private sector – but the workers involved are not locals anyway, they mainly come from Australia and New Zealand. It is clear that some ethnic groups have a strong tradition of public sector work, and others very little. It is hard for one council to change these factors. There is another issue, rarely broadcast on the left as being too embarrassing: there have been in some areas a few individuals who used their 'minority' status to abuse their positions as officers engaging in wholesale skiving, endless complaints and grievances, persecution of managers who are merely trying to do their jobs, and so on. Such abuses can only discredit attempts to deal with genuine issues of disadvantage in the public sector or elsewhere.

In the light of the past decades of run-down and privatization, Paul's interesting ideas for the expansion of democratic local services into new areas such as energy, water or estate agency seem crazily optimistic. Yet globally, at different times, public/collective bodies have effectively provided local services of almost every kind at some time. Paul is right to suggest that local projects on energy, economic and environmental issues were among the most productive features of the 1980s local socialism, and to a limited extent they continue in Britain and on the continent.

While the defeats of the left in the 1980s and later privatization and cuts in the 1990s have blocked off a lot of potential, more qualitative aspects of turning the local state outwards, involving communities, decentralization and such have often been able to continue. Not everything New Labour does is totally bonkers. Value for money, client satisfaction, community consultation and equalities input are now pretty much taken for granted in the public sector. It is true there has not been as much devolution of money and power as ideal, but as stressed above there are inherent dangers in this, which Paul rather naively ignores. It may be that, as he suggests, radical councillors wasted much money in the 1980s – even the best-intentioned libertarian socialists can be incompetent with cash, I don't doubt. The old guard's scepticism may have been justified. He is right in suggesting that 'bureaucrat bashing' is pointless and that the left often sought a quick fix where there was none, and that councils and other bodies are staffed with individuals with hopes and fears like us all. The folk you need to carry out reforms do need to be brought along with you and not annoyed by endless reorganizations or bringing in whizz-kid supremos from outside.

Moreover, Paul is spot on in identifying the centralist and anti-pluralist nature of much of the old Labour Party and the old left. The last fifteen years have seen this concentration of power and suspicion of local communities and front-line staff only accentuated under New Labour and its 'modernization' agendas. This has led to even backbench and opposition councillors being cut out of the loop, let alone staff and residents. Where services have been outsourced wholesale to companies like Capita and S.I.T.A., or to housing associations/care providers, even the pretence of democracy and consultation disappears. As he puts it, everybody else had to change except them – this is true a fortiori of the new-wave Blairite municipal leaders. Like the worst aspects of the old guard left, they are sure they alone embody the peoples' interests whatever the latter say – as in endless attempts to foist privatization or stock transfers on tenants who clearly don't want it. A sceptical Blairista asked one councillor in a neighbouring borough about the success of stock transfer. Did the tenants like the new arrangements? "No idea" - quoth the councillor – "Not our problem any more."

This is the point. Paul may be right that local government has lost its radical potential and we should go back to building up bases in civil society among communities, tenants and disadvantaged groups. Still, the problems in recent years have not been the accrual of power within the local state but the loss of these powers to unaccountable quangoes and private companies documented by George Monbiot and others.

5. Frankie Ashton: Autonomous Movements And Alliances

At this point I move on to territory where I may make myself somewhat unpopular for challenging some of the received wisdom of *Chartist* – especially our 1980s politics. For some, there is no basis for a white, male Anglo Saxon able-bodied person (and trainspotter at that!) to have anything to say at all about movements and aspirations of groups who may be disadvantaged in our society. They are invited to fast-forward at this point.

My basic disagreements with Frankie's very interesting contribution are two. The first is that she implies, like many 1980s radicals, a view of modern Britain where ethnic minorities are systemically repressed by society in a way reminiscent of apartheid South Africa; while gays and women are also suppressed across the board, if not to the extent of contemporary Saudi Arabia. The second issue is that these matters of what has been called 'special oppression' are conflated with movements connected with peace, the environment and so on – clearly a different matter altogether as such movements are open to any and everybody to join.

Her perspective is summed up in this quotation: 'Just as reformism is incapable of realizing socialist goals, because it fails to redistribute power, wealth, opportunity and outcome, so too is a class-based socialist strategy alone, incapable of liberating the diversity of oppressed interests in our society.' Well, just as orthodox socialists have sometimes downplayed the real advances made by the working class within capitalism, so writers like Frankie Ashton in the 1970s and 1980s seem to have missed some major trends in society. We have lived through twenty-seven years since Thatcher came to power in 1979. Whatever the ideology of politicians and capitalists in the 1980s, the world was changing rapidly. The right did lauch a real class war against working people as a whole and the unions in particular. Most laws protecting workers were repealed and replaced by ones that persecuted them. Unemployment soared; whole areas of the country written off, while social inequality rocketed.

Yet there were no moves to repeal legislation on race or sex discrimination: in fact gender equality is now hard-wired into the whole E.U. by statute. As for gays, the celebrated symbolic Clause 28 made no difference to anybody. In the early twenty-first century, the Tory party is competing with business groups and establishment organizations like the church for plaudits in being gay friendly, anti-sexist, and anti-racial discrimination. This is a far cry for the days when 'loony left' councils were lampooned in the tabloid press for wanting homosexuals to have equal rights. At several points,

Frankie suggests that capitalism is trying to exclude women from waged work, as if we were back in the 1950s. This is remarkable in the view of the massive feminization of the British workforce since the 1970s. It is the old 'white male' strongholds of the print, the docks, the shipyards and the mines that Thatcher shredded. It is men who, if anybody, have been excluded from the workforce: older men with redundant skills in the British rustbelt, young men with nil education left adrift by the collapse in demand for unskilled labour. Clearly, it is in the public and service sector that this has grown fast, and not just Polly Toynbee's army of 'carers, cleaners and caterers'.

None of the above implies that we have arrived in some kind of egalitarian, 'right-on' paradise; but the British society really has moved on dramatically since the 1950s, although these changes will have been much less obvious back in 1990 when Frankie Ashton wrote. True, in the U.S. the religious right and other conservatives have fought a strong rearguard action against gender and ethnic equalit. The left will get taken seriously by nobody if it goes around pretending that the world isn't what it is and that hard line racism or 'patriarchy' are inseparable from capitalism. The more equality in other areas is achieved the clearer the real basic fault lines between the wealthy minority and the rest of us are revealed.

Where Frankie is quite correct is demolishing simple-minded leftists who used to think all oppression is just a subset of class. A moment's reflection indicates that a wealthy capitalist woman can be abused by her partner; bigots can attack gay or Asian capitalists. What needs to be separated are two concepts: on the one hand the oppression and bigotry of civil society, on the other what is fashionably described as 'institutional racism'. The first is clearly widespread, though most folk are neither extreme bigots nor thoroughly politically correct. You only need to sit in a back street South London local to hear plenty of throwaway racist remarks; no doubt if you taped what black or Asian citizens said in their clubs and bars you would find similar prejudice or dislike. Opposition to mixed relationships does not just come from white society, for instance. Similarly, violence against women and gays continues to be commonplace – maybe even more so in the less enlightened provinces. However this does not equate to 'institutional racism' or institutional sexism, which implies something ingrained or systemic in large entities beyond the attitudes of individual officials. I suspect that there is a lot more institutional oppression in the private sector, especially in manufacturing or small firms or places like the City of London. Yet it is usually the public sector that is raked over the coals and seems to be present in so many industrial tribunals. I surmise this is because the public sector is much more open to scrutiny, has to follow detailed rules, allows unions to monitor events, and is unable to sack staff just because their face doesn't fit.

These points are made because Frankie Ashton's prescriptions only make sense in a flawed and outdated view of the world. Socially and culturally, the broad working class is diverse and fragmented. Gender and race play a role here, especially in particular employers or workplaces if certain jobs are seen to be reserved for men, whites, or whatever. However, is this typical of the workforce as a whole? Are these differences really less than those between full and part-time staff (who may both be women), permanents and temps, managers and subordinates, professionals and routine employees, those who stagnate and those who are fast tracked?

It is one thing to defend women from rape or violence by their partners, another to imply that some forms of dress, behaviour or family set-up are more desirable than others. It is one thing to defend ethnic minorities from physical or verbal abuse and from discrimination based on their origins, another to lay down the law on 'multiculturalism' to the extent that it is supposedly not OK for public bodies to celebrate Christmas or Easter in a country that has been at least nominally Christian for thirteen hundred years, or to suggest that every document or sign be translated into minority tongues, or that all religions have totally equal status. Frankie talks of 'arranging' such matters as housework and childcare, moreover of working to replace marriage and the nuclear family by some unspecified collectivism. She and other feminists are perfectly entitled to such aspirations and whether any of us happen to agree is hardly the point. The question is whether it is the role of the state or political parties to seek to re-arrange peoples' lives in this way. Those in charge of the state might reflect that the nuclear family has already been much eroded in recent decades, not towards any utopian lifestyle but in the direction of social breakdown and anomie.

Many members of the public have deeply held views against abortion or homosexuality. So long as women can have freely available terminations and gays/lesbians enjoy comparable status, there is a limit how far it is desirable for society to impose its own concepts of what are acceptable views to express. When it comes to female circumcision, the point is the non-voluntary nature of it in most cases, in a situation where a common sense interpretation of multi culturalism implies a laisser faire attitude by society. I suppose if a woman wanted this revolting procedure done a free society would have to let her, though it sticks in the throat.

There is also the issue of the 'social movements' that Frankie refers to. The word 'social' implies something more than coteries of intellectuals and activists. It is true that the organizations of the left and of labour often represent on a day-to-day basis only a handful of enthusiasts (though at least some seven million voluntarily choose to join unions). Similarly, there is not in any meaningful sense a 'Women's Liberation Movement' per se. What there are of course are innumerable individual women influenced by modern feminism and active in all kinds of organizations and movements as well as in workplaces and professional bodies. Moreover, there remain campaigns on particular issues such as rape that do brilliant work, like the equally marginal (numerically) left campaigns on civil liberties, nuclear weapons and the like. I have no wish to criticize these bodies, about which I know very little. They may well have achieved much more than the left has since 1979. Nevertheless, can they be said to 'represent' the views and interests of women any more than the Communist Party or the S.W.P. 'represent' the interests of the working class?

When it comes to ethnic and religious groups, the situation is rather different. There is little doubt that, in many cases, the groups represent quite a lot. The S.W.P. has put the strategy of 'alliance' into operation by dissolving the Socialist Alliance into Respect along with the Muslim Association of Britain. At a local level there have been many cases of groups being set up claiming to represent this or that ethnic community. It would take a lot of effort to find out exactly how representative they all were. In a political sense, what do you do? Ally with all of them? In many cases, there may be fierce factional squabbles even within one ethnic community, let alone between say, Sikhs, Hindus and Muslims in Southall or Handsworth. In practice the strategy of alliances depends so them all being worthy left-aligned (C.P. influenced) bodies like the Indian Workers Association of old. However, if the left says it will ally with black or Asian groups, so long as it agrees with their policies, where is the 'autonomy' of these movements?

The point is not that groups representing minority communities are a bad thing, certainly not in respect to newly arrived groups where many members lack awareness of how things work and have limited command of English. Without such groups, it would be very hard for local councils, doctors and other agencies to do their work in many cases. However, does that make the promotion of such groupings an end in itself, beyond immediate needs to combat whatever discrimination and abuse exists? If the norm is that members of these communities retreat into some kind of voluntary ghetto rather than joining forces with others in unions and political parties, this might be seen as a sign of lack of progress not the reverse. It may be that I have distorted Frankie's views here, but it is unclear from the published text what these alliances might mean in practice.

Frankie also deals with 'issue' politics such as the peace and ecology movements. These raise a very different set of issues. Peace movements, especially regarding major issues like Iraq, are by definition single issue campaigns and it makes absolute sense to build them as such to encourage the widest participation from those of all political or ethnic backgrounds. This is so-called 'tactical promiscuity'. The bigger the movement in which socialists engage, the better are the chances to make our feeble voice heard.

When it comes to ecology the case is different. Environmentalism is not really an autonomous movement. On one level, it is a series of dilemmas posed at society which are being faced across the board by politicians of the right and centre, by civil servants, and business groups. Many would argue that free market and business-led solutions are the way to deal with environmental problems. On the other hand, the Greens are a political and para-political movement of the soft-to-radical left, sometimes congealing as a formal political party but rarely limited to only one. Environment groups of the grass roots type, at least, are broadly part of the active left constituency the same as ourselves. Most of their activists are leftist, both by disposition and affiliation, quite rightly too. The issue is not how 'Green' leftists ally with the mainstream left bodies so much as how both move out of our current ghetto existences. Just as the left only gets support when it abandons all or nothing 'socialism tomorrow' - type ranting for pragmatic reform strategies, so the Greens will be marginalized if they are seen as demanding an instant renunciation of all the lifestyles of western consumerism and affluence, a tightrope indeed.

6. Mike Davis on 'The Third Road'

Mike was writing this after three Tory election victories, when the Thatcherite hegemony seemed unshaken, even if the lady herself was in the process of being strapped to the ejector seat by her colleagues. He was absolutely right to draw attention to the 'defeat, demoralization and crisis' on the left at the end of the 1980s. It would be nice to think we had recovered ground since, but in many ways the effect of Blairism has been a further wave of defeat and pessimism on the left, plus a desertion in the direction of neo-liberalism by some coteries of ex-socialists. I think he takes too much at face value the 'moral majority' side of Thatcherism and its 'Victorian' appeals for hard work and sacrifice. The reality had a lot more to do with the lure of easy dosh (epitomized by Harry Enfield's Loadsamoney character) and something for nothing (privatizations, council house sales); however this is by the by.

Mike refers to the dilemma about whether the working class is dwindling or merely being reconstituted, an area where the pamphlet as a whole seems to face both ways. In general, he sums up very well the consensus *Chartist* had arrived at by 1990. Simple-minded Leninism and stodgy Fabian reformism were to be rejected. Concentration on economic and workplace issues was to be supplemented by cultural and ideological insights (following the work of Gramsci) while socialists would ally with the best of the new social movements that Mike saw as growing rapidly - to some extent the reaction to Thatcher made them do so. Socialism had been discredited by its monolithic, top down or authoritarian persona. In some respects, the analysis is flawed. It was true that the traditional (i.e. manual) working class was in decline, but this was not the main reason why Labour kept losing. 1980s Labour did pretty well at building a base among clericals and professionals, especially in the public sector – it was Thatcher's success in winning over many 'blue collar' households that was the real problem.

Mike correctly draws on the discussion begun by Eric Hobsbawm's book *The Forward March of Labour Halted* but draws inadequate conclusions. He implies 'labour' has failed because it was too sectional and the left too 'economist' – therefore one must bring on new alliances of some kind with the 'pluralist' movements mentioned above which would presumably appeal to a broader audience. As suggested above, this begs a whole load of questions. It implies that the left or the labour movement is somehow 'over here' while these movements are somehow composed of different individuals 'over there' – perhaps feminists, ecologists, black or Asian groups, peace campaigners and so on. Even at the level of activists this is dubious – in reality there is a broad progressive moment in Britain as in many other countries, some of whose activists are more involved in unions, some in green campaigns and others in issue campaigns – but are nonetheless a broadly similar sub-culture who read the same papers/magazines, watch the same TV, meet in the same pubs or whatever. However, getting fifty folk wearing different hats together in one room is not really the point. The problem is that the union activists cannot deliver the union members, the feminists can't deliver the women, and most of the ethnic minority groups cannot mobilize more than a small proportion of their constituency. The fundamental problem was (and is) the general isolation of what have usually been radical intellectuals from the broader culture and movements in current society.

This is not to say that the strictures of Mike Davis and co are irrelevant. No doubt, it would have been better if the old labour movement had been less easily stereotyped as being manual, white, male and all the rest of it. On the other hand, some of his prescriptions for unions getting more pluralistic sound a bit like unions becoming political parties, which is hardly what most of their members join them for. Often it is hard to win arguments for union participation in the political arena even on bread and butter issues, except among unrepresentative cliques of activists masquerading as mass movements. In my view the fundamental problem for the political left was that the folk it represented – organized labour in shorthand – had been rolled back, defeated notably in the great 1984/85 miners' strike and also at successive elections under the ludicrous British voting system.

Leftist politics inevitably seems a lot more plausible when the constituency it represents has a significant weight in politics and society, just as free-market dogma only moved outside college seminars when the bourgeoisie began its big fightback in the 1970s. No doubt, new thinking would have been a good idea. Back in the 1960s and 1970s the limitations of old style social democracy had surely been 'exposed' under Wilson and Callaghan; however so had the dead end of mindless militancy. This was typified by the reaction to the Bullock proposals on industrial democracy, sunk by an unholy alliance of American-type business unionism (Frank Chapple et al) with the unreconstructed hard-left. The proposals may have been flawed but they would surely have represented a great step forward.

There was more to the 1970s and 1980s left than this. Excellent discussions took place around seminal ideas like the Alternative Economic Strategy and the Lucas Aerospace Alternative Plan – a kind of Third Road politics in practice. Mike rightly points out the potential strength of this kind of thinking. Unfortunately, it was largely confined to subsets of the soft-left and did not permeate either the ordinary grass roots union membership or the political activists steeped in electoral or other routines. By the time such ideas had become current the broad-left, still dominated by blinkered thinking, had been forced back into its box for the duration – and in 2006 its remains are still there. This is important to stress. The idea that the left is bereft of ideas is risible. The shelves of radical bookshops - the few that exist - have groaned for decades with worthy tomes on all sorts of aspects of modern society and economy. Some may be dogmatic rubbish or the 'big bang' school of socialism, but much has been intelligent, progressive, thoughtful and outgoing.

However, it is hard to imagine that small groups of activists, no matter how marvellous their analysis or however inclusive their tactics, could have had much of an effect during the long periods of leftist electoral defeat during the last twenty-five years.

This sounds gloomy but class struggle "hasn't gone away, you know" - not the caricatures of militant shop stewards and the like, but the sordid everyday reality that big business using the fig leaf of so called 'globalization' is aiming everywhere to cut back the earnings, social benefits and political rights gained by working people across the western world from the 1940s to 1970s. The idea that working people were bought off by the system isn't daft. If the system gives you rising living standards and social security, why rise up in militant revolt with uncertain chances of success for a future that may not be very nice?

It is true that there is nothing unproblematic about any development of pan-working class consciousness or solidarity, as the expansion of the workforce (in the U.S. from around eighty to hundred and thirty millions in the past thirty years alone) has coincided with a fragmentation between part and full-timers, temps and permanent staff, professional, manuals and clericals, managers and subordinates – but outside the rose-tinted spectacles of simple-minded leftists was this ever not the case?

What Mike says about 'pluralist' alliances with the newer social movements allied to class and socialist perspectives is fine. This should be seen not as some shotgun marriage between workers and alien forces from elsewhere, but alliances between different wings of the same progressive movements. Sure, there can be ecologists, gay activists, ethnic groups, peaceniks or feminists who are in other respects on the right wing of politics. Why shouldn't they be? It is highly patronizing to suggest otherwise. In most cases they will probably be marginal but we don't need to have any hang-ups with allying with them in a good cause (such as against Blair's Iraq adventure). After all, even the far-right Alan Clark M.P. was hot on animal rights and the like. The real issues are not so much the assumed opposition between workers and blacks or women but issues such as the environment. Clearly modern capitalism has engineered an utterly unsustainable lifestyle whereby everyday patterns of travel, heating or consumption are in violent conflict with the long-term health of the biosphere, maybe with the survival of humanity.

Nothing is more central to our vision than the nature of modern capitalism that has swept all before it. Well, up to a point. Actually, modern capitalism bears scant relation to the free market daydreams of the Adam Smith Institute and the like, which does not stop many on the left believing their fantasies. In sordid reality Smith's *Wealth of Nations* (1776) described an idealized fantasy of how the economy could be organized, not what was going on in a Britain industrializing under mercantilist (state-sponsored) management. Hence the huge scale of import duties and the smuggling business of the time; hence the need for a decades-long campaign to repeal the Corn Laws. Later countries that came along were more state-sponsored still, from Germany and the U.S.A. to South Korea and Taiwan. Neither the state capitalism practiced in Europe and the Far East nor the state collectivism of China and similar regimes bears much resemblance to the academic free market model of the Invisible Hand.

In the western heartlands, it has been clear for decades that capitalism socializes the means of production as conventional Marxists have long predicted. A few decades ago Jack Cohen could start with a couple of stores and build up a retail empire. Nowadays his Tesco has well over thirty percent of the retail market, most of the rest going to another three or four big chains. There is no chance at all of a small company breaking into the supermarket game. There are two possibilities: free market competition continues until Tesco and one or two competitors have complete dominance with effective regional monopolies, or else the state intervenes to cap the growth of these firms and even break them up. The latter would of course be an artificial state-managed competitive market, with firms being prevented from expanding naturally, effectively being granted limited franchises by the state in the same way as bus or train operating companies are allowed to run contracted out public services. Microsoft is the real extreme – whoever heard of competition in the software market, when almost anyone who buys a new machine finds it pre-loaded with Mr Gates's products?

I do not necessarily relish this position. Indeed I find the disappearance of family-run local breweries pretty depressing. Nevertheless, it is the reality of our time, and socialists should start from realities not fantasies. In eighteen years, the Tories ran down and sold off major public services, but the share of public spending in the national economy fell only by a few percentage points. There are just too many social and infrastructure overheads for modern capitalism: education, healthcare, pensions, roads and railways. A lucky minority can afford to look after themselves but most of these services will inevitably be provided by the state directly or indirectly. The issue is about what basis this will happen on, under whose control and for whose benefit,

This is why I am sceptical about 'anti-statist' rhetoric. It is true that some state services have been oppressive, monolithic, bureaucratic, even corrupt. However, their creation was for real historical reasons not some free-floating ideology. The Attlee government may have justified its nationalization and welfare state measures as being 'socialist', but conservatives, liberals, Christian Democrats and fascists (in Italy) were doing similar stuff for quite pragmatic reasons. Most European railway systems have always been state-run, or state-guided. In England there was a genuine free-for-all leading to the construction of numerous duplicating routes between major centres, to the endless fascination of enthusiasts: this was the exception, not the rule. Big industries were taken over by the state because individual capitalists lacked the money or the motivation to create or modernize them. Hence the need for bourgeois parliamentary regimes whose cadres are often NOT business types (they are too close to things) but more detached – progressive aristocrats in nineteenth century Britain, social democrats and the like in more recent times.

For that matter, state collectivism on the Soviet model took off largely because radical leaders saw statism as the road to crash industrialization and social/technological progress for their countries.But socialism without popular control and democracy is meaningless, however benign the dictatorship. On the other hand, it is stupid to dismiss the state as just oppressive and reactionary. There are clearly modern models, for example Scandinavia, where advanced and educated societies have used state intervention to modify and house train capitalism within certain limits.

The danger is that in reacting against the simplicities of the old left, critical socialists like *Chartist* have been tempted to throw out the baby with bath water and make similar criticisms of so-called heavy-handed state bureaucracy to Thatcherites and Blairistas. Most folk in the modern western world are oppressed by big business not by the state bureaucracy, whatever its failings. Mike uses the phrase 'enabling state' which New Labour uses to justify wholesale privatizations and transfers to quangoes and the like – unaccountable bureaucracies with no popular input at all. To ask 'how much power should the state have?' is wrong – in the modern world the state will have massive power and influence in some form or other, if we define it broadly, even in so called free market societies like the U.S.A. The real question is: 'who has power over the state?' George Monbiot talks of the 'Captive State'. Our model needs to be of a state and an economy both decentralized and broadened out to popular and democratic pressure (not just well organized activist groups).

What of the future? Mike outlined a range of radical alternatives to the traditional centralist left that bear repeating. Unfortunately, they focussed on the idea of a revitalized, decentralized, activist and pluralistic Labour Party, working through central and local government structures but in alliance with trade unions and all the progressive social movements discussed above. As we know bitterly enough, the past fifteen years have seen the reverse – the suppression of most of the independent thinking and democratic practice in the Labour Party under the Stalinist regime of the New Labour faction, combining the worst aspects of old guard communism and labourism. The party structures have been hollowed out to a husk, dominated by brain-dead terminal loyalists and smarmy careerists often with a foot or two on the rungs of patronage. It is ironic that Mike argues at one point for a downgrading of the union link - however bureaucratic the block vote system – since nowadays the union presence is almost the sole vestige of progressive politics in the Labour Party. He did not seem to appreciate fully how a small elite can manipulate an individual membership party unless strong democratic safeguards are hardwired in; even had they been, power and wealth can sidestep them. Blair and his court dominate Labour by patronage and bullying, simply ignoring the formal democracy which exists increasingly on paper.

As long as the central state and the main parties are so dominated by neo-liberalism and corporate interests, the excellent proposals for radical local grassroots democracy outlined here will only exist in a marginal way. Instead of a proliferation of housing co-ops, we get the forcible transfer of council housing to the so-called voluntary sector: in reality, the housing associations are just a glorified set of quangoes with no accountability whatsoever. While Mike's criticism of union sectionalism and wage claim economism may be fair enough, insofar as they really took on all the social and political agenda he advocates, they might be in danger of turning themselves into alternative political parties. This would be fine if it was what most of the seven million union members joined them for, but I rather doubt this is the case in current conditions. As for worker co-ops, some recent privatizations involved management buy-outs (e.g. bus companies) with the shares being spread among the workforce. At the first opportunity, they generally sold out to Stagecoach or whoever. From a short-term point of view, this may have made some sense. I would like to say that co-operatives have been a raging success globally, but with some exceptions (North American credit unions) they have in recent decades at best been able to manage secular decline in influence and resources, however noble their aims and methods.

Mike ends with a generally excellent justification of the traditional critique of capitalism and outlines the kind of participatory and pluralist socialism that should find wide appeal. In some respects, he may be a bit pessimistic. When he says there is no mass support for 'socialism' it depends what is understood by this. There is not a lot of support for the tepid technocratic reforms of past Labour governments. However, when Blair abolished Clause IV an opinion poll showed over a third of respondents agreeing to it! (Clause IV said nothing about state control of anything, by the way.) I suspect across Europe there would be a lot of support for a populist, pragmatic reform socialist agenda that would benefit the mass of the population at the expense of the privileged elite. The trouble is that usually only discredited ingrown sects like the old Communist Parties advocate such policies.

Leftist politics must be based on the consciousness and hegemonic side. Ideas in peoples' heads really do change the world, as do contingent 'events, dear boy, events', as Marx would be the first to acknowledge. We cannot ignore the overall ideology of the time, or the state of morale in the workers' movement. On the other hand nor should we ignore socio economic reality. Neo-liberalism (alias globalization) has only worked in a very narrow way, entrenching the privileges of the very wealthy. Overall, growth rates since the 1970s have been less than in the Welfare Keynesian period from 1945 to 1974. In the developing world things have mostly gone backwards since developmentalism was replaced by marketization. Even in the few western countries that have superficially done well, like the U.S., the process has been accompanied by massive polarizations in income, galloping insecurity, social anomie, and unsustainable economic imbalances such as debt bubbles. Neo-liberalism is an ideology that covers both social and economic failure. Its more crazed adherents, as in Britain, fail to understand the extent to which modern capitalism is utterly dependent on increasing the role of the state, not a return to an Adam Smith dream world of the night watchman state.

7. Conclusions:

Fifteen years ago, comrades from *Chartist* and our friends in Clause IV spent many hours working on the *New Maps* project. We felt, rightly, that it distilled the main areas of a critical programme and critique towards revitalizing the drooping traditions of the left within Britain and beyond. It is right that, now we are addressing a rather different world in the early twenty-first century, we should look back the strengths and weaknesses of our previous analyses and see where we might have been misguided before.

Overall it stands up pretty well. Everything we said about the uselessness of the old Leninist and Fabian technocrat traditions has been richly borne out. It was hard to predict just how irrelevant most of the old hard and far-left would become, or how social democrats would turn from promoting social control over capitalism to zealously presiding over the marketization of the public sector and welfare services. It has to be admitted that the 'Third Road' debates we participated in never got very far. Rather than spreading outwards as we optimistically hoped, the further erosion of the life of the left and Labour Movement under Major and Blair deprived us even of a significant audience for our views. In recent years one has cynically felt that even if we got progressive socialist proposals adopted by the T.U.C. or the Labour Conference, what bloody difference would it make? Most of those who have understandably given up activity in rent years have not defected to the far-left or even the worthy Green Party; they are just sitting a decade or two out. Only leftist parties that have developed a relation to mass popular or workers' movements - as in parts of South America - can win significant election victories, even get onto the political map. Even well known radical intellectuals and 'champagne socialists' like Pinter or David Hare seem becalmed by events. The absence of effective charismatic populist figureheads for our movement is significant too – think of the role of Chavez or Morales in South America!

In 1990, Trevor Fisher penned his concluding chapter ('Mapping the Future') at the height of the American and capitalist self-congratulation with the collapse of the old Soviet bloc. This was epitomized by Francis Fukuyama's triumphalist book *The End of History?* We were all supposed to believe that free-market capitalism and U.S. style liberal democracy were going to carry all before them for ever and ever. Naturally, Trevor's stance was cautious and defensive but as he put it, '… traditional reformism and Leninism have entered a cul de sac and show little sign of back tracking.'

Fifteen years later, one feels Trevor could have been a lot more robust. As for the collapse of the state collectivist regimes, the idea that societies where a few dozen gerontocrats on the Politburo take all the big decisions could be socialist is absurd. Whatever the positive sides of the Iron Curtain countries, they never had a hope once they had suppressed popular democracy. Not only was it undemocratic, it was unplanned (unlike modern capitalist corporations!) as the plans largely existed on paper. Across Eastern Europe, hardly anyone sprang to the defence of collective state property even in 'self-managed' Yugoslavia. As for the capitalist 'victory', there has been scant economic revival, though a few multinationals have set up manufacturing facilities to take advantage of cheap labour. Most of Eastern Europe has hardly recovered to the output of 1990 and some areas like Russia are way below it. Living standards and welfare benefits have plummeted for all but the wealthy new elites. Death rates rise as birth rates decline.

Meanwhile in the West, neither the free-market nor the interventionist economies have done particularly well despite the absence of Communist competition. They have defeated their internal lefts and labour movements and restored profitability, but based on stagnant investment and finance-led economic bubbles. Countries like Germany and Japan have strong economic fundamentals but increasingly feel unable to give their citizens the same benefits their parents had after the War. As for the English speaking powers, collapse into hubris is only a matter of time. The 'American Century' looks increasingly unlikely given the shambles in Iraq and the huge twin deficits overshadowing Bush's nirvana.

In overall terms the socialist critique has surely been vindicated in the last fifteen years. Yet few apart from eccentric academics and fringe sects ever make this point. However, the alternatives have been marginalized. 'Third Road' politics never really got off the ground in Britain. The similar Eurocommunist strategies in Spain and Italy were first contaminated by their links to Moscow totalitarianism and then dumped as Stalinists followed social democrats into capitulation to neo-liberalism. Other parties like the French C.P. kept to their principles but declined into sects.

Such has been the decline of even the most promising left parties (like Swedish or Austrian social democrats) that it is hard to feel short-term optimism. The kind of progressive un-dogmatic thinking we have argued for in *Chartist* will be of little use confined to university seminars or debates in small rooms over pubs. Yet the broad labour movements of previous decades can in the short term do little until revived by an influx of new blood and breaking from the old hard left shibboleths of the early twentieth century. It is true that few nowadays waste their time arguing about who said what in 1917 or 1938, but are they arguing about anything relevant instead? Too many of the best socialists seem to have followed Voltaire's *Candide* ('Il faut cultiver notre jardin') in the face of the marginalization of the left. It is true that there have been fantastic revivals of protest over Iraq, civil liberties, globalization and welfare cuts in many western countries. Unfortunately, these have not yet translated into ongoing active movements, nor have they won more than the odd skirmish. At least there are now shelves full of sensible and original left thought not just on a critique of the status quo but stating alternative strategies and social models: co-ops, participatory budgets, electronic networks, environmental sustainability, and the like. Recent election victories in Latin America show the Washington Consensus is not as invincible as many imagine.